HOBOKEN'S LACKAWANNA TERMINAL

By THEODORE W. SCULL

QUADRANT PRESS, INC.
19-WEST 44th STREET
NEW YORK, N.Y. 10036
(212) 819-0822

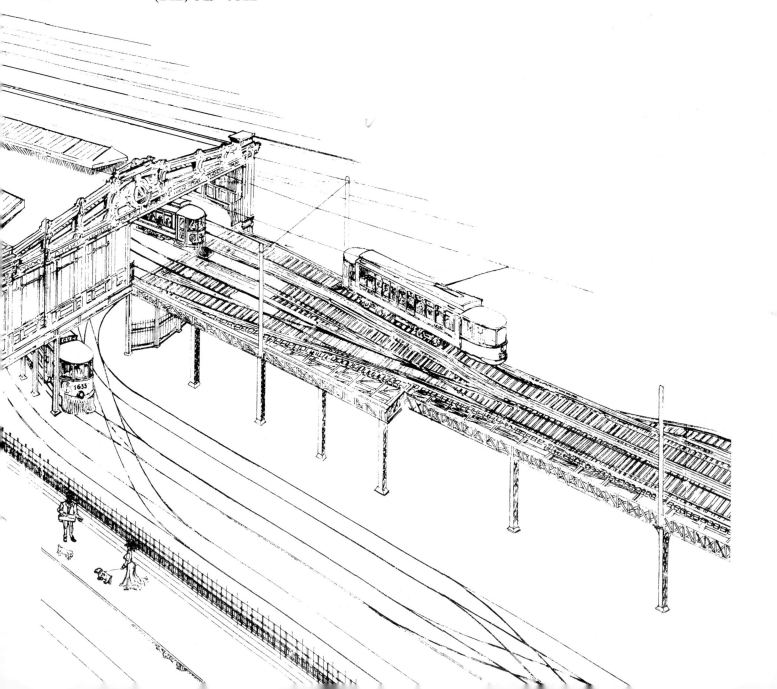

INTRODUCTION

Hoboken could be variously described as an island, the end of the line and a way station to someplace else at almost any period in its nearly 350 years of recorded history.

Geographically, the Hudson River, vast tidal marsh lands and towering palisades defined the place, separating Hoboken from the interior, from the other river landings to the north and south and from Manhattan Island, Hoboken's main focus and impetus for rapid development.

On the east, the river remained Hoboken's most visible boundary even after the arrival of the cross-Hudson ferries and the construction of the vehicular and railway tunnels. From the west, roads crossed the swamps and railways tunneled under the palisades ending Hoboken's relative isolation. They would eventually create man-made boundaries, with sprawling railroad yards to the south and sweeping highway approaches to the Lincoln Tunnel to the north. Hoboken remained a kind of island, roughly a mile square.

As a major transportation center, Hoboken became an important place where people began and ended their train journeys, ferry rides, ocean liner voyages and car and bus trips. While local Hobokenites greatly benefited from the highly developed riverfront, rail and road network, the vast majority of passengers were simply passing through, to and from New York.

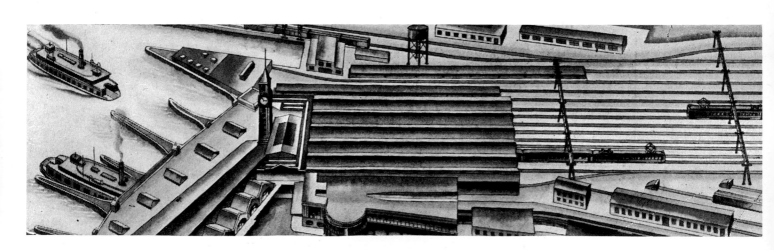

In this aerial photograph taken prior to World War II, the extensive Lackawanna facilities are to the left; the city of Hoboken is laid out neatly to the right; Jersey City rises behind the Palisades and the Meadowlands stretch across the top. Beyond the terminal the Pullman, Hill and Day's yards are full of passenger coaches, and the puffs of white smoke indicate steam locomotives idling and on the move. The terminal's clock tower points directly up to the Observer Highway trolley trestle leading away from the terminal and angling into Jersey City. In the left-hand corner, the marshalling yards can hold up to 3000 freight cars, and on the waterfront, lighters, barges and tugs line the Long Slip and Piers 1-6. (Wes Coates Collection)

The ferryboat Elmira, dating from 1905, slides gracefully towards her Hoboken slip with a load of hatted commuters on April 17, 1961. (Conrad Milster) In the spacious lower cabin, homebound commuters enjoy their newspapers in the kind of roomy comfort that no other means of transportation could ever offer. (Fielding L. Bowman)

The afternoon rush hour is about to begin in this 1923 scene. The commuter train consists are long enough that many of the locomotives await beyond the train shed. Smoke obscures the landmark clock tower, normally visible for miles in every direction. The Lackawanna Railroad's commuter trains helped develop the suburbs of northern New Jersey, providing an excellent service that had one of the best on-time records in the industry. (D. L. & W. photo by W. B. Barry, Jr., John Willever Collection) 54 years later in 1977 a Hoboken-bound electric approaches Millington Station on the Gladstone Branch. (Fielding L. Bowman)

The "Twilight Limited," passing through Morristown westbound in July 1952, gave business people almost a full day in New York before heading to stations in the Poconos and the Southern Tier of New York State. A dining car ran through the dinner hour as far as Binghamton, and the parlor served stations west to Corning. In the mid-1960's the author used the train on Friday nights, after slipping away early from work on Pier 40, to ride to Cresco for a weekend with his aunt who lived in the Poconos. By the end of 1965, the train and its friendly diner-lounge were gone. (Homer R. Hill)

The Delaware, Lackawanna and Western Railroad and its subsidiary, the Hoboken Ferry Company, had by far the largest impact on the riverside community together spanning more than a hundred years of service. All good stories have a climax, and for the Lackawanna Railroad and the city of Hoboken, it had to be the years 1905 through 1907.

Early in the morning of August 7, 1905, a great fire swept away the old wooden ferry house and railroad station in a matter of hours. Less than two years later on February 25, 1907, a new Lackawanna Terminal combining function and beauty rose from the ashes to become the finest combined waterfront railroad and ferry complex anywhere in the world.

Both the railroad and the city had made it into the big leagues with a transportation cathedral that overshadowed all the others along the New Jersey shoreline.

More than one hundred thousand travelers a day passed through the terminal to ride the Lackawanna's impressive fleet of white ferryboats for New York or to board the railroad's steam-powered trains to the nearby suburbs, the rich coal mines of Pennsylvania, the Pocono resorts or westward into the heartland of America.

Arriving by ferry at one of the six slips aboard a stylish double-ended steam ferryboat, passengers passed beneath curved arches of ornamental copperwork into a vast upper level concourse with massive columns supporting a roof punctuated with rectangular skylights. Wide sloping ramps led them to the lower train concourse, and a grand staircase gave entry into a waiting room 50 feet high, illuminated with dripping chandeliers and decorated by a ceiling of colored Tiffany Glass and rich plaster ornamentation.

On the far side of elaborate iron gates stood fine trains like the steam-powered "Lackawanna Limited," with a well-known reputation for burning clean anthracite coal, and a whole fleet of commuter trains that helped develop northern New Jersey's bedroom suburbs and rural communities from the Oranges to the Delaware Water Gap. Within the train shed long rows of fluted ionic columns held up an innovative design of low-flying canopies that kept out the elements and dispersed unwanted coal smoke.

Local streetcars, horse carts and private vehicles pulled into the ferry house forecourt bringing passengers and produce to a lower-level entrance separated from the upper-level concourse through which most of the heavy pedestrian traffic using the trains passed to reach the ferries. There were three Manhattan destinations from which to choose; Barclay Street for the financial district and the Washington Market in Lower Manhattan, Christopher Street, directly across the river in the West Village and West 23rd Street, the main approach to what in 1907 was midtown Manhattan.

Today, Hoboken's ocean liners, long-distance trains and trolley cars are gone forever, and the ferries, perhaps only temporarily. But a visit to the terminal at 8 o'clock in the morning will reveal a surge of humanity that has continued largely unchanged. NJ Transit electric and diesel commuter trains disgorge thousands of commuters at one time who then make a beeline for the underground PATH trains to Manhattan or for connecting buses or go on foot to school or work nearby.

During the day and on weekends the terminal relaxes its pace, only to gear up again for the 5 o'clock assault during the homeward rush.

The terminal's railroad portion retains its vital function and much of its beauty thanks to landmark status and a federal grant, while the ferry house languishes unused, dropping bits and pieces of its ornamental facade into the murky waters of the Hudson.

The active Lackawanna Terminal has outlived its neighbors on the Jersey side of the Hudson: the West Shore Terminal at Weehawken, the Erie at Pavonia, the Pennsylvania at Exchange Place and the Jersey Central at Communipaw. With the sole exception of the magni-ficently restored Jersey Central Terminal, sadly without trains or tracks, all the other waterfront structures have been demolished, leaving open scars in their place waiting for some future non-transportation development.

Unlike Grand Central Terminal and Pennsylvania Station, located in congested Manhattan settings where the design is so sophisticated that the trains are invisible from the main concourse, the Lackawanna Terminal's trains are lined up beyond the original iron gates waiting to be seen, heard and ridden by all who approach. There is something quite raw and wonderful about the place, a railroad terminal where appearance and function are inseparable.

As a result, several films, including "Funny Girl," "Three Days of the Condor," and "Voices," plus numerous TV commercials and print advertisements have used the Lackawanna Terminal and its trains for their location.

When I first came to New York 21 years ago, I used the Erie-Lackawanna ferries and long-distance trains to reach the Poconos on weekends until they were no more. The commuter trains have taken me numerous times to Bernardsville, Morristown, Montclair, Suffern, Tuxedo and Port Jervis and nearly always on time.

More recently, when I began to make a serious study of this wonderful place, I had a chance to talk with some of the people who work there, to explore the terminal's interior, climb across the roof and delve into original source material. I have had the opportunity to show off the Lackawanna Terminal on walking tours, and now I am happy to share the story of its history and design and its ferries and trains.

Theodore W. Scull
New York, Summer 1986

Pre-revolutionary Hoboken, like Manhattan across the river, first had successive settlements of Indians, followed by a very brief Dutch period, and finally, the British. By the time of the Revolutionary War, Hoboken already had a primitive and irregular ferry service, and it was considered strategic enough to be fought over, with victorious British troops occupying the site during most of the period of the hostilities.

After Independence, the relatively few travelers arrived mainly by stagecoach over the Paterson Plank Road laid across the soggy New Jersey Meadowlands and the Passaic and Hackensack Rivers. If someone arrived too late for the last ferry of the day across the Hudson to the Corporation Pier at the foot of Vesey Street in Manhattan, he could spend the night at the 1776 House, located where the present bank building at Hudson and Newark Streets is today. Several blocks of landfill have since enlarged Hoboken in much the same way Lower Manhattan has been added to.

Travel between New York and Philadelphia became a highly competitive market, with stage lines, steamboats and ferries vying for their share. Ferries to Manhattan had long been established from Paulus Hook (Jersey City) across the Hudson, through the Upper Bay from Staten Island and over the East River from Brooklyn.

Some ferries were simply rowing boats for passengers, and others were sail-powered flat-bottom canal

CHAPTER I
EARLY HOBOKEN

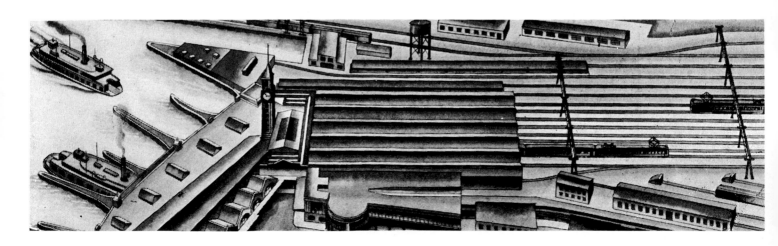

Hoboock Ferry   1775

boats for transporting heavy loads. The most reliable and elaborate ferries were the team boats or horse boats propelled by mules or horses turning a treadmill connected to a paddle wheel mounted between two parallel hulls. Some team boats had two paddle wheels and three hulls lashed together.

Colonel John Stevens invented the team boat and ended up having to use it even after he developed his own working steam ferry in 1811. Stevens, a wealthy financier and inventor with excellent connections as the result of serving as Treasurer and Surveyor General of New Jersey in the Revolutionary War, bought the square-mile area of Hoboken in 1784 for $90,000. To develop his parcel of real estate opposite Manhattan, he needed to establish a regular ferry service with a predictable crossing time, one that was not possible in a sailing or rowing boat subject to the vagaries of wind and tide.

The team boat, though quite slow with the pace of a good walk, could keep a schedule, and wagons could be driven on at one end and straight off at the other without unhitching the horses or turning the boats around. In other words, Stevens had invented the first double-ended ferryboat.

In a very short period of time, Col. Stevens connected a steam engine to side wheels and launched the "Juliana," the first steam ferryboat in the world, named in honor of his daughter. On September 18, 1811, the "Juliana" made its maiden trip from Hoboken to Vesey Street, and five days later completed eight round trips with an average of 100 passengers on each crossing. To allow boarding at any stage of the tide at the Vesey Street pier, Stevens developed a set of float-

One of the earliest known views of the Hoboken (also Hoboock or Hoebuck) Ferry in about 1800. The 1776 House overlooks the landing where the sail ferry Peregaus is moored. (Romance of the Hoboken Ferry)

A Horse Boat in 1815

This 1815 horse boat is an early example of a trimaran, a three-hulled open flat boat where teams of horses provide the power to turn the two paddlewheels. (Romance of the Hoboken Ferry)

9

Powered by a sidewheel walking beam engine, the Fairy Queen of 1826 had a long life on the North River shuttling between Hoboken and several Manhattan ferry houses. (Romance of the Hoboken Ferry)

By the early 19th century the landing at the foot of Barclay Street became an important approach to Manhattan's business district and the Washington Market. Here a steamboat line operating up the Hudson (or North River) shares the crowded waterfront with a deep sea sailing packet and the ferry to Hoboken. The building at the right sells tickets for the Paterson Stage Line running from the ferry over the Plank Road in New Jersey. (Drawn by C. Burton, Engraved by J. Smillie, Museum of the City of New York)

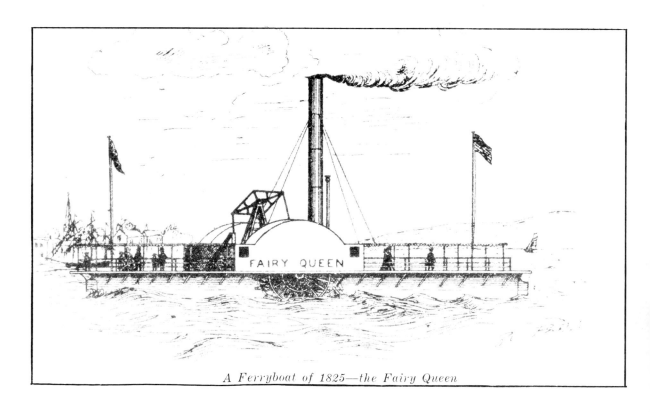

A Ferryboat of 1825—the Fairy Queen

Drawings dated March 10 and June 2, 1866 depicting the chaos that reigned at the Barclay Street Ferry during busy travel times, before the separation of wheeled conveyances, animals and foot passengers. Frank Leslie's Illustrated Newspapers, Courtesy of the Hoboken Public Library)

ing stairs that rested on a pontoon, the forerunner of the more sophisticated floating transfer bridge.

After a winter lay-up, the little "Juliana" had successful 1812 and 1813 seasons, after which the Legislature of the State of New York gave Robert R. Livingston and Robert Fulton a monopoly to navigate the Hudson with boats propelled by steam or fire.

In spite of this temporary setback, Stevens ran a thriving business using team boats on a route to Spring Street from 1813, and to Vesey Street, briefly switching to Murray Street and finally becoming firmly established at Barclay Street by 1818. Canal Street service began in 1823; and then, as New York City gradually moved northward, a permanent landing was created at Christopher Street in 1838. Spring Street service ended in 1825 and Canal Street service stopped in 1864.

When the Livingston-Fulton monopoly ended, Stevens established the Hoboken Steamboat Ferry Company in 1821, and within a year had the Stevens-built 100-passenger ferry "Hoboken" running every hour on the Barclay Street route. The 98-foot, 9-knot boat, using pine as fuel, could make the crossing in about 20 minutes.

In 1823 Stevens' new ferryboat "Pioneer" was innovative in more than name, for this fast boat boasted a mirrored and carpeted ladies' cabin below the main deck, heated by an open wood fire. Ladies' cabins, in a somewhat altered form, continue right up to the present-day Staten Island ferryboats. The Barclay Street Ferry now had half-hourly departures.

The steam ferry became firmly established when the 1826 "Fairy Queen" was placed on the Canal Street run, replacing the last of the team boats.

In 1823, an elaborate rate sheet spelled out almost every imaginable item and form of transport that might cross the transfer bridge, remaining in effect for thirty years. A passenger ticket cost 12½ cents; a market wagon with one horse and one driver 37½ cents, and the same wagon with four horses one dollar. The rate for a mahogany chair read two cents but for a common chair only one cent. Various rates were set for a large Pennsylvania wagon, a coach, coachee, chariot, two-wheel carriage, phaeton, sleigh, pleasure wagon, covered wagon, chaise, top chair and sulky, depending on the load, the number of horses, passengers and drivers. The majority of people today would need a good dictionary to identify most of these mysterious and now forgotten conveyances.

The rates appear high today, and they were, for in 1853 the ferry was losing so much money that the tariffs for nearly every category were drastically slashed. The fare for foot passengers, aged ten and over, fell to 3 cents, in line with most of the other cross-river services.

In the interim, the Stevens family turned its attention to developing Hoboken's real estate potential by establishing the Hoboken Land and Improvement Company in 1838. Its goals were to lure the major international shipping lines across the river and to build an exclusive residential community, with access to jobs in local waterfront industries and in Manhattan by means of the ferry.

About this same time, a fledgling railroad, using the nearby Erie Railroad tracks, linked Hoboken with Newark, where it connected to the Morris and Essex Railroad, incorporated in 1835. The M & E soon stretched across New Jersey on a route through Morristown, Dover and Hackettstown, reaching Phillipsburg by 1866.

Hoboken incorporated in March 1855, and the regular and generally reliable ferry service had much to do with the city's growing accessibility. In the fall of 1850, permanent night service began on the Barclay Street run, an important breakthrough in the availability of 24-hour transportation.

For mid-19th century New Yorkers, Hoboken may have been best known for its Elysian Fields, a popular landscaped riverfront playground. Frederick Law Olmsted's Central Park had yet to be finished, and Manhattan's rapidly growing urban population was beginning to run out of breathing space. Women and their small children came across the river during the weekdays in warm weather, and whole families descended on Hoboken on the weekends, especially on Sundays.

Frank Leslie's Illustrated Newspaper on October 11, 1856, praised the pleasures of Hoboken:

> Nature, in all its kindly freaks, never designed a prettier place than Hoboken, none more sweetly commingling hill and dale, prairie and precipitous rocks, water and land together. Happy indeed was the name of Elysian Fields.

The well-laid-out park boasted fine views of the river in a relaxed sylvan setting with paths to stroll, cool water to drink and picnic grounds in which to enjoy lunch. The first regular game of baseball was played here on June 19, 1846.

Visitors from Manhattan arrived by ferry and then followed River Walk for about a half-mile to Elysian Fields, beginning at 5th Street, passing beneath 100-foot high Castle Point and ending about 17th Street. By 1860, the weary could take a horse car on Washington Street, Hoboken's main north-south artery then and now.

An 1867 map showing Hoboken's street grid, Elysian Fields and the German steamship piers. The Morris & Essex Railroad makes its approach along the border with Jersey City to the site of the 1862 station and the ferry slips for Christopher Street and Barclay Street. (Taintor's Route and City Guides, City of New York, 1867)

To draw the large crowds over from Manhattan, the Hoboken Ferry began to advertise heavily in the local newspapers in a manner found in this example dated November 1856:

> The Commodious and very swift new Ferry Boats, Paterson and Chancellor Livingston, are now plying regularly on the Barclay Street Ferry, leaving each side punctually every fifteen minutes during the day, viz: at the even hour, half hour and intermediate quarter hours, crossing the river from seven to ten minutes, according to tide. The Ferry Boats to Canal and Christopher Streets, each leave twice an hour from Hoboken. A Night Boat runs (all night) to Barclay Street. New and spacious Ferry Houses at Hoboken, Barclay and Canal Streets.

However, an article entitled "The Hoboken Ferries," appeared in the morning edition of *The New York Herald* dated Monday, September 7, 1857 that reported the ferry services from a different perspective:

> The ferry being the principal breathing outlet to the city, especially for women and children, who desire to take a sail during the warm weather, and the thousands who daily visit Hoboken, of all sexes and ages for pleasure, it is something to be regretted that the present owner of the several ferries, Edwin A. Stevens, Esq. does not take more active measures to provide against any accident or emergency which is so liable to arise at any moment, especially on boats so continuously crowded as those with women and children . . . . Not one of the seven boats employed on the Barclay Street, Canal Street and Christopher Street ferries are anything like adequately supplied with life savings implements . . . . The Phoenix is said by those who should know to be unsafe, and entirely unfit for use as a ferryboat. So dangerous is she regarded by many who are familiar with her, that they prefer walking to Canal Street, and crossing to Hoboken by that ferry to risking their lives on board this boat . . . . On the Hoboken side carts and wagons are driven in every direction and at haphazard, inside of the gates promiscuously among the passengers, rendering it anything but agreeable or safe for foot passengers, especially during the busy periods of the day."

There appear to be two different criticisms here. One concerns the safety of the boats and the other, the separation of traffic at the ferry houses. It would not be until the 1907 terminal that most of the passengers and freight moved on and off the ferryboats at different levels.

The ferry fleet did comprise, by the mid-1850's, some first-generation ferries that were more than 30 years old and undoubtedly due for replacement. Fire took the "James Rumsey" in 1853, and government service in the Civil War acquired the brand-new "Hoboken" of 1861, soon to be lost in the Burnside

Expedition. By the end of the war, a new generation of ferries came on line but this was not to be the end of subsequent fires and collisions lasting well into the early 20th century. However, considering the tens of millions of passengers who used the ferries, the safety record in terms of injuries and deaths was an excellent one from the 1880's onward.

The ferries not only served visitors and local Hoboken residents but formed the water connections between Manhattan and the Morris and Essex Railroad. Between 1862 and 1885 there were four wooden Hoboken rail terminals, separate from the ferry houses, each one larger than its predecessor to handle the railroad's growing passenger and freight business.

The first terminal lasted only from 1862 to 1868, when a larger one was constructed on filled-in marsh land and offered a covered walkway from the train platforms to the ferry slips. The second terminal was destroyed by fire in 1873, and its replacement was only meant to be a temporary structure. When the Delaware, Lackawanna and Western Railroad was able to run through same-gauge trains over the Morris and Essex and directly serve Hoboken, the track rights over the competing Erie on their line under Bergen Hill began to become the source of friction.

The D.L.&W.'s own tunnel opened in May 1877, severing any connection with the Erie for the next 79 years. The fourth terminal, with three joined wooden sheds covering eight tracks, opened in 1885, and its destruction by fire 20 years later cleared the way for the present "fireproof" Hoboken Terminal, completed in 1907.

The 215-foot ferryboat Secaucus-completed in 1873, had a particularly long life on the North River, lasting until 1920 when the boat was sold to the Carteret Ferry Company, finally burning in 1935. The Hackensack, built in 1871 to almost the same specifications, had a shorter life. A checkered career saw the boat rammed twice by an Erie Railroad ferry, finally becoming "stranded and bilged at Sunken Meadows on February 12, 1897." (F/B Secaucus - Bill Rau Collection; F/B Hackensack - F. R. Hathaway Collection, Courtesy of the Steamship Historical Society, University of Baltimore Library)

The ferryboat Bergen, completed in 1888 at the considerable cost of $135,835, became the first single shaft, screw propeller, double-ended ferry in the world. The boat could operate at a speed of 12½ miles per hour, being both faster and more economical than the sidewheelers of the time. The shaft drove two props, one pushing and the other pulling, while the ferry was in motion. The elimination of the paddle boxes, as seen on the steamer Rosedale at the right, allowed for 30 per cent more passenger space. The Bergen had her gas and oil lamps converted to electricity in 1906, and the ferry lasted 65 years until finally scrapped in 1953. (Museum of the City of New York)

In a space of 50 years, the small railroad serving Hoboken via a tenuous connection over a foreign road and a transfer in Newark grew into a major coal hauler, produce carrier, and passenger company having New York as its main market and linking up at Buffalo to the western rail lines and the Great Lakes steamer operations.

The Lackawanna's suburban service received high marks from the 1893 edition of King's *Handbook of New York City:*

> The Morris & Essex Division gives access to the most beautiful of all the suburbs of New York, the villages around the Orange Mountains, the Oranges, Montclair, Summit, Short Hills and Morristown, whose pure highland air and pleasant scenery are widely celebrated. The suburban traffic on this division has assumed great proportions, and is yearly increasing, on account of the desire of New-York business men to keep their families and to spend their own leisure days in the beautiful region of New Jersey, where the climate is of such sovereign salubrity that people are sent hither, even by physicians in Europe, as to a sanitarium. The suburban train-service is kept up to the highest point of efficiency, and affords the best of facilities, whether one goes northward on the route via Passaic and Mountain View, or westward by Newark and Orange, Summit and Madison. Largely on this account, the region of the Orange Mountains, so richly endowed with landscape-beauty and pastoral charm, has become perhaps the favorite residence-district in the outer suburbs of New York, and presents the aspects of a great park, adorned with hundreds of pleasant county-seats and dozens of dainty hamlets.''

There seemed to be little journalistic dissension when it came to the early Lackawanna suburban service, in sharp contrast to reports about the ferries.

The Hoboken Land and Improvement Company wanted a share of the lucrative international shipping trade and shore front support facilities such as shipbuilding repair yards, coal piers and iron and machine works.

As overseas and coastwise oceangoing freight and passenger business outgrew the East River docks, it began spilling over into Brooklyn, then up the Manhattan side of the Hudson; and, finally, some large steamship lines crossed the river to the New Jersey side locating on the strip of waterfront due north of the Hoboken Terminal.

In the late 1850's two rival German lines, the North German Lloyd sailing to Southampton and Bremen and the Hamburg-American Steamship Company with services to Southampton and Hamburg, took up residence side by side at the foot of First and Second Streets. The ships brought a large German population, some of whom established thriving shoreside businesses that served the lines. Large numbers of Italians and Irish soon followed, making up the three major ethnic groups by 1900.

Located just north of the Hoboken Ferry were the new piers belonging to the North German Lloyd, sailing to Bremen, and the Hamburg-American Steamship Company, sailing to Hamburg. The three large ships are sail-assisted early steam packets, with the one docked next to the pier marked 'Bremen', most likely the 2,674-ton Bremen of 1858, NGL's pioneer ship on the North Atlantic, able to make the Western Ocean passage in 12-14 days. (Frank Leslie's Illustrated Newspapers, Saturday, October 30, 1858. Courtesy of the Hoboken Public Library)

Below, the 17,000-ton first Nieuw Amsterdam had been in service only five months when this card was mailed from Boulogne, France to St. Paul, Minnesota on October 6, 1906. To the left of the Holland-America liner is the brand-new Day Line side-wheeler Hendrick Hudson, and to the right of the tug flying the N.A.S.M. flag is the Lackawanna ferry Netherlands built in 1893. Right, in a similar setting the 19,000-ton North German Lloyd liner Kaiser Wilhelm II, the world's largest in 1903, is flanked to the left by a Pennsylvania Railroad ferry and to the right by a tug flying the company flag and other North River ferries, including appropriately the white Lackawanna ferry Bremen. (Both post cards - Herb Frank Collection)

HARBOR
SCENE
NEW YORK

1904. ILL. POS
CARD CO., N.Y.

T.S.S. NEW AMSTERDAM. Oct 6-1906.
Love + best wishes
HOLLAND-AMERICA LINE. W. P. A.

Fifteen years later the Netherlands-American Steam Navigation Company, forerunner of the Holland-America Line, arrived, remaining a fixture for over 90 years at the Fifth Street Pier. Thingvalla Steamship (later the Scandinavian-American Line), the Phoenix and Wilson Lines rounded out the early companies that helped bring Hoboken to its peak of prosperity, filling every inch of the waterfront with maritime activity.

With the shipping facilities stretching northward further away from the established ferry services at the Hoboken Terminal, an Upper Ferry at 14th Street was opened on May 3, 1886, operating across the Hudson at one of its narrowest points to 14th Street, Manhattan.

The terminal was at first not well served by connecting transportation, and there was surprisingly little patronage for the first few years. The ferry operated every half hour during the day and hourly from midnight to 7 am, and there were reports that the boats often shuttled back and forth empty with the gates never opening.

The heart of Hoboken was nearby the Lackawanna Terminal, while the northern end of town was relatively undeveloped. Local traffic from Jersey City to Hoboken and to the ferry increased with the completion of the Ferry Street (Observer Highway) railway trestle in 1886. This elevated line was a great improvement over

The small ferry house at 14th Street Hoboken first served 14th Street Manhattan until 1904 when the ferry moved north to 23rd Street. The building was replaced by a new and larger structure in 1928. (Courtesy of the Hoboken Public Library) The plans for the Fourteenth Street Hoboken Ferry date from 1903, the year the D.L.&W. acquired the ferry operation. Note the Public Service trolley tracks that approach the north side of the terminal from the left. (D.L.&W. official plans)

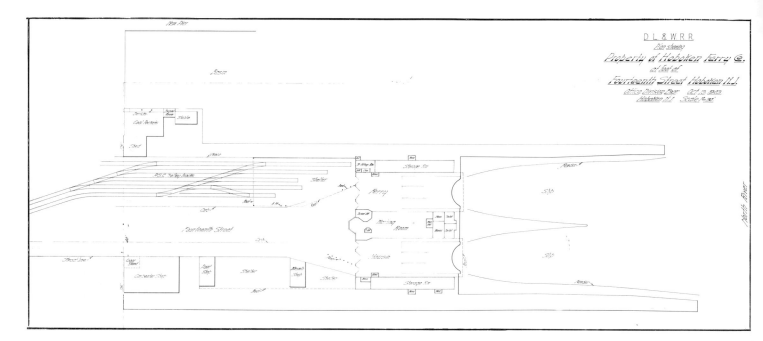

the cumbersome incline that had hauled traffic up the palisades to Jersey City Heights since 1874. Trolley lines also ran north to the West Shore Line Terminal at Weehawken, Palisades Amusement Park and several other destinations.

Substantial small-city public buildings sprouted along the main streets leading from the terminal and ferry house. City Hall construction began in 1879, was completed in 1883 and then enlarged in 1910 and 1911. The Hoboken Free Library was dedicated on April 5, 1897, and both buildings survive today. Stevens Institute, established 1870, and the Stevens family castle dominated the hill and headland above the river. In 1910, Hoboken reached its peak population of 70,324. Today's figure is 42,000 (1984).

Hoboken's most illustrious watering spot in the late 19th century was The Duke's House, a restaurant and bar located just back from the ferry slips, ideally situated to attract the rich and famous from Manhattan. Two fires and changing times ruined the place, and today only a remnant dating from 1935 can be seen, and its days are numbered.

In the last 20 years of the 19th century, Hoboken grew rapidly in importance and 1) the City Hall, 2) the Free Library, 3) the Clam Broth House, and 4) the row houses on Washington Street, between 3rd and 4th — note 'Hoboken' and 'New York' at the top of the cornice — have all survived to today. (All photos - the author)

Probably better known to people living today is the Clam Broth House, opened in 1899 just two blocks from the present terminal and still going strong, though the clientele is now decidedly more local.

At the turn of the century, Appleton's Dictionary of New York, 1902, described Hoboken in these words:

> Hoboken is a continuation of Jersey City northward along the Hudson River, but it is still an independent municipality, and, as the State of New Jersey does not display the same anxiety to make an imposing showing of large cities as New York, it will probably remain so for some time to come. Hoboken is a suburb of New York City, very popular with the Germans, who form the bulk of the population. It stretches along the foot of a steep hill which rises within about half a mile of the river front . . . . Along the edge of this hill (where stands Stevens Castle and Stevens Institute), with the river bank on the right, is a promenade to Elysian Fields, formerly a fine pleasure ground with stately trees and luxurious grass, but now sadly neglected and all but ruined . . . . German beer gardens abound in Hoboken, but they are not so well kept as they should be to attract other than purely local custom.

Central Park removed the need for the extensive grounds of Elysian Fields, and increasingly Hoboken became a waterfront city with all the smoke, congestion and habits that go with such a function.

In 1900 a major conflagration swept Hoboken's North German Lloyd property, and in 1905 two fires, only months apart, completely destroyed Lackawanna rail and ferry facilities on both sides of the river.

The most serious one, known as the Great Hoboken Pier Fire, began in the afternoon of June 30, 1900 in some cotton bales stored at the land end of Pier 3,

View down the "L" Road Trestle, Jersey City to Hoboken, N. J.   8-11-07.
Arrived this eve, 5 o'clock, will write soon. Best wishes. Is. E. J.

Once considered the largest wrought iron structure in the world, the EL Road carried cable cars then electric trolleys between the Lackawanna Terminal and Hudson County Court House in Jersey City and other routes, from 1886 until the last day of service on August 7, 1949.
(Bill Rau Collection)

2209--Elevated Road to Jersey City Heights. N. J.

Souvenir Post Card Co., New York and Berlin.

Christopher Street Ferryhouse, 1888

The Christopher Street ferry house served as the innovative New Jersey Pavilion at the Philadelphia Centennial Exposition in 1876. A single steel girder supported the roof shaped like a circus tent. A year later it was bought by Edwin Stevens and brought piece by piece on barges to New York where it was re-erected between the Inman Line's Pier 43 and the White Star Line's Pier 44, both transatlantic steamship companies serving Liverpool. (Romance of the Hoboken Ferry)

The ferryboat Musconetcong and its sister Hopatcong, both just short of 200 feet long, were a pair of walking beam sidewheelers costing $40,000 each that entered service in late 1885 on the Christopher Street Ferry. It was the captain of the Musconetcong who first spotted the fire aboard the Hopatcong on the night of August 7, 1905. While the Hopatcong was destroyed, the Musconetcong lasted until 1923 when it was sold for $85,000 to the Westchester Ferry Company for the Yonkers-Alpine run and renamed F. R. Pierson. Note the reverse sheer and the very large camber to the top of the superstructure. (Capt. Parslow Collection, Steamship Historical Society)

Ferry passengers are watching the Great Hoboken Pier Fire of 1900. The four-funneled North German Lloyd liner Kaiser Wilhelm der Grosse has been towed safely away from the conflagration, while the smaller, not-so-lucky, twin-funneled Saale is burning from stem to stern. (Courtesy of the Hoboken Public Library)

setting afire the North German Lloyd liner ''Bremen'' (1897). The flames quickly spread to the adjacent piers where the liners ''Kaiser Wilhelm der Grosse'' (1897), ''Main'' (1900) and ''Saale'' (1886) were docked. The ''Kaiser Wilhelm der Grosse'' was towed into the middle of the river and saved. The ''Main'' and ''Bremen'' ended up beached off Weehawken, heavily damaged; and the ''Saale'' drifted downriver and grounded off Ellis Island, ending up completely gutted.

The final death toll came to between 200 and 400 souls (an exact count was never known), many unable to escape through the tiny portholes and included passengers, visitors, crew and longshoremen. Some were burned to death, while others died of smoke inhalation and drowning. While the ''General Slocum'' disaster in 1904 claimed many more lives, and the 1942 ''Normandie'' fire is remembered by more people, the Hoboken pier fire directly involved more ships and more lives.

The fire that destroyed the ferry house and fourth Hoboken Terminal began aboard the ferryboat ''Hopatcong'' just before midnight on August 7, 1905. Before the ferry could be pulled from her slip the ferry shed caught fire and eventually the entire transportation complex burned to the ground. The ''Hopatcong'' was beached at Weehawken where the ferry became a total loss, burning to the waterline. Fortunately, the brand-new ''Binghamton,'' which also caught fire, was saved by her crew and rebuilt, and in the end has survived them all.

After the fire, the Hoboken ferries continued to use the slips but the Lackawanna passenger trains terminated at Newark, and passengers were routed to other waterfront terminals or used the Public Service

Two post card views of the last wooden ferry terminal at Hoboken. The land-side view shows the entrance for teams for Christopher Street to the left and Barclay Street to the right. Foot passengers were encouraged to use the smooth paving stones in the center to and from the passenger waiting room but in practice they walked where they wanted to. The second view from the river shows three of the white ferryboats. One is the Montclair, the last walking beam sidewheel ferry, completed 1886. (Bill Rau Collection)

Arthur Livingston, Publisher, New York 584

HOBOKEN FERRY, HOBOKEN, N.J.

The Lackawanna Limited is about to make its daily 10 a.m. departure from an earlier Hoboken Terminal at the turn of the century. (Mountain and Lake Resorts on the Lackawanna Railroad, published by the Passenger Department in 1903, Howard Samelson Collection).

23

A color postcard showing a twin-stacked fireboat battling the Hoboken fire at the D. L. & W. Terminal. The card was posted by a New Jersey mother to her daughter in Lewiston, Maine in October 1906. (Howard Samelson Collection).

FIRE BOAT IN ACTION NORTH RIVER, D. L. & W. R. R. HOBOKEN FIRE

tomorrow night we take one of the boats for New Jersey after a day's sight seeing in New York Love to you all Mama

One post card shows the new ferry Elmira unloading passengers shortly after the fire. Construction has already begun on some temporary structures to the extreme left and right. The other scene is to the left of the ferry slips and depicts the ruins of the Duke's House, Hoboken's most noted night spot frequented by the rich and famous from New York. The landmark restaurant bar, though rebuilt, never recovered its reputation after the fire. (Both post cards - Bill Rau Collection)

ENTRANCE TO HOBOKEN FERRY AFTER FIRE, 8-7-'05.

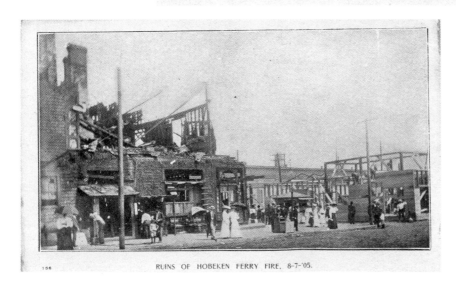

RUINS OF HOBEKEN FERRY FIRE, 8-7-'05.

24

Virtually nothing remains of the wooden ferry terminal in this photo by the D.L.&W.'s official photographer the day after the August 7, 1905 fire. The two Public Service trolleys run to Union Hill and Summit, the latter a principal stop on the Lackawanna's Morristown Line. (D.L.&W. photo by W. Barry, Jr., Homer Hill Collection)

trolleys for a few days until the rubble was cleared away to allow a resumption of connecting train and ferry services.

On December 20th several painters putting finishing touches on some pipes underneath the new West 23rd Street ferry terminal started a small fire that spread quickly, fanned by high northerly winds, destroying both the Lackawanna and Central of New Jersey facilities. At the height of the conflagration the clock atop the 100-foot high tower stopped at 10:55 am, and one-half hour later fell over into the street. To the North, the buildings belonging to the Erie and Pennsylvania Railroads were spared.

Ironically, the Lackawanna had only moved its ferry services here from 14th Street a year before. The four railroad ferry operations made West 23rd Street the second most important transportation terminal, after Grand Central, in the city.

The replacements for the burned facilities on both sides of the Hudson became marvels of their age, a pair of splendid Beaux-Arts-style ferry houses, featuring impressive clock towers, and one fine railroad terminal that surpassed all others on the New Jersey waterfront.

A foggy day down by the river on the day after the fire that destroyed the almost new 23rd Street ferry house. Everything made of wood burned leaving only the collapsed steel structure. The fire lines still crisscross the terminal's forecourt. Passengers were directed to nearby slips to the north for their boats over to the Lackawanna Terminal and to 14th Street Hoboken. (D.L.&W. photo by W. B. Barry, Jr., John Willever Collection)

CHAPTER II

THE LACKAWANNA TERMINAL OF 1907

The extraordinary waterfront terminal that rose from the ruins of the previous wooden railroad station and ferry house was the culmination of a master plan that combined innovation, practicality and magnificence on a monumental scale. The Lackawanna's more than 100,000 daily patrons could now transfer from the ferries to the trains and to connecting local transportation with ease and safety without ever going outside, and do it in an atmosphere of elegance and beauty.

Where most of the Hudson River frontage presented an unsightly hodgepodge of structures and styles, the new 730-foot Lackawanna Terminal gracefully united its several functions into one interconnected facility, with a copper exterior that glistened during the day and shone brightly under powerful illumination at night. Large signs with letters four and six feet high beckoned local Hobokenites to the North and Manhattanites from across the river. More lights outlined the ferry house arches and pillars facing both the river and public square. People in all compass directions could tell the exact time from one of the four self-winding clocks set high up on the 225-foot tower housing a 2,500-pound bell and rising from the terminal's flat roof. In the maze of lights from the shoreline facilities, liners, tugs and ferryboats, the illumination of the Lackawanna Terminal must have presented an orderly pattern along the cluttered Jersey shore.

Kenneth Murchison, a Brooklyn-born New York architect, developed the design for the combined railroad terminal and ferry house. He graduated from Columbia University with a doctorate in 1894, studied achitecture at the Ecoles des Beaux-Arts in Paris for three years and then returned to New York to establish a private practice that lasted 32 years. Undoubtedly, his Paris experience inspired the Beaux-Arts classical design for the Lackawanna Terminal, his finest work. That city brimmed over with examples of the style in its public buildings and private residences.

After establishing his reputation with the Lackawanna Terminal in 1907, he would go on to design other railroad stations in Baltimore, Scranton, Havana and Jacksonville; as well as important office and bank buildings, hotels and hospitals. He died in December 1938 at the age of 66.

The Delaware, Lackawanna and Western was first and foremost a railroad with New York the primary focus for the company's growing freight and passenger business. The freight side comprised such diverse cargoes as coal, grain, fresh fruit and vegetables, milk, and mail and express, all requiring specially designed

The 225-foot clock tower rises from the roof of the ferry house concourse just behind the pitched roof of the main waiting room. Below, passenger coaches occupy the tracks adjacent to the Bush Train Shed. Above the roof of the Pullman and Immigrant Building the ferryboat Montclair approaches Slip 1. Modifications to the 1886 sidewheeler allowed for upper deck loading, an important feature of the new terminal. To the extreme left, the stacks of one of the North German Lloyd liners can be seen. The photograph was taken from the roof of the new powerhouse still under construction. (D.L.&W. photo by W. B. Barry, Jr., Homer Hill Collection)

The Delaware, Lackawanna & Western Railroad Terminal, Hoboken, N. J., 1907

handling facilities. The bulkier items arrived on freight trains that used the marshalling yards to the south of the new terminal for transfer to barges and car floats for the crossings to Manhattan, Brooklyn, Queens and the Bronx.

All the other traffic was destined for the tracks adjacent to the main terminal. Milk trains arrived at several tracks next to the Express Building to the north of the passenger yards; and the mail cars went directly to a waterfront structure at the terminal's south end for transshipment, mostly to New York. Virtually all long-distance passengers from Scranton, Buffalo and the West and daily commuters from the New Jersey suburbs transferred from their trains to the ferryboats for Manhattan.

The ferry fleet, however, received only half its foot traffic from the trains, with the other half arriving on electric trolleys, in motor vehicles and on foot. In addition to passengers, the ferries carried wheeled conveyances of all kinds on their main decks, from passengers' baggage and mail carts to horse-drawn produce wagons and early motor cars and trucks.

Inland railroad-owned land was more plentiful than the relatively short stretch of waterfront available to the Lackawanna for funneling all this diverse traffic across the river. The new terminal's plan used separate approaches, one-way ramps and sets of stairs connecting two levels to handle the movement, much of it concentrated within a few short hours in the morning and afternoon.

The most obvious requirement was to divide access to the ferry between the train passengers and everything and everybody else. Earlier reports illustrated the chaos resulting from the failure to separate people and wheeled conveyances, not only in Hoboken but at ferry houses all along the river.

Hence, the ferry house, instead of being sited directly at the end of the terminal tracks, was angled to partially abut the railroad station while it also opened onto a large forecourt to receive the non-railroad traffic. The result was a layout entirely unique in waterfront terminal design.

To prevent the entanglement of railroad passengers and vehicles, train travelers were encouraged to pass from the train concourse to the ferries by means of ramps and stairs to an upper pedestrian ferry concourse and onto the ferry's saloon or upper deck. Even people arriving on the streetcars and on foot passed into an enclosed waiting room in the ferry house's lower level, where, after paying their fares, they were also drawn up by a convenient set of stairs to board the boats above the freight traffic.

Not only was the flow of all types of traffic carefully planned; but, in the event of an interruption in the ferry service, the train and ferry concourses, the waiting

The canopies spanning pairs of tracks and single platforms are clearly evident in this 1910 photograph looking east toward the ornate clock tower that rises from behind the main waiting room. The radio tower to the right was used to communicate with the trains during their runs to and from the terminal. (D.L.&W. photo by W. B. Barry, Jr., Homer Hill Collection)

The drawing shows Kenneth Murchison's Lackawanna Station in Scranton, Pennsylvania, remarkably similar to his Beaux-Arts Baltimore Station built for the Pennsylvania Railroad in 1911. The Scranton station is now a Hilton Hotel while the Baltimore station, restored in 1983, is Amtrak's fifth most important and also receives commuter trains from Washington. (Drawing by Bartlett, photo - the author)

Virtually the entire span of Lackawanna Railroad passenger and freight facilities is visible in this remarkable photograph taken from the river shortly after the terminal was opened in 1907. To the right are the new ferries Scranton (1904), Ithaca (1906) and part of the older Bremen (1891). Dead center is the famous restaurant with a striped canopy shading the outdoor dining area. To the left of the immigrant slip is Pier 1 where a D.L.&W. lighter is tied up. (Museum of the City of New York)

rooms and ramps could hold up to 20,000 (some crush load estimates go as high as 40,000) people without overcrowding or creating the danger of spilling back onto the train platforms and into the street.

The entire terminal building and parts of the train concourse and public square rested on a concrete platform supported by wooden pilings over the water. The bulkhead line ran almost parallel to the front of the ferry house, then continued diagonally beneath the station concourse and the ends of Tracks 13 and 14.

The pilings, 80 to 90 feet long and made from yellow pine, were submerged two-thirds of the time, and as they never dry out because of continual tidal action, they will not deteriorate with age. To protect the building from damp rising through the floor from the river, the entire foundation was insulated by three layers of felt and one of coal tar pitch.

The steel and concrete structure needed to be flexible enough to allow for uneven settlement and to be able to withstand the shocks caused by the ferryboats when docking. Today, both the floor of the train concourse and the terminal's waiting room show an irregular surface where sections have sagged over the years.

Edward Thoden, Engineer, Structures, today regularly inspects the foundation in a small boat that enters the underside of the terminal through one of the ferry slips. He times his travels to coincide with sufficient water and an ebbing tide so he is sure of getting out.

The use of wood and other combustible materials was

This pair of photographs shows construction crews taking time to pose during the building of the terminal in 1906. In the background is the skeleton of the main waiting room and clock tower, and to the right is a nearly completed section that will house the ramp leading from the upper ferry concourse to the train shed, upon which the four men are seated. In the second photo, the men are resting on one of the steel beams that run along the top of the columns used to hold up the canopies. (Howard and Suzanne Samelson Collection)

kept to an absolute minimum to prevent the recurrence of the disastrous fires that continually plagued waterfront facilities. The plan used wood sparingly as a nailing surface for copper ornamentation, but only under the cornices and gutters, for the transfer bridges in the ferry house and for the racks that the ferryboats used for docking. The offices had wood trim and wooden floors, but most of the furniture was made of metal.

Fireproof doors separated storage areas and offices from the enclosed public spaces. The elaborate firefighting system consisted of wet fire lines and standpipes winding throughout the terminal, with high pressure turret nozzles on the roof that could reach the entire building surface.

The air-cooling system was one of the first installed in a major building in this country. Electrically-operated paddle fans circulated the air, chilled by huge

blocks of ice, through a network of ducts to all interior spaces.

The rich copper ornamentation on the outside surfaces gave the building a Beaux-Arts metallic texture in varying shades of green that changed over the years. The copper sheets were formed in the workshops into a myriad of architectural shapes, reinforced with iron riveted onto the back side and then bolted to the concrete surfaces. To create green and brown patinas, the copper was dipped into acetic acid solutions. Age has now erased many of the subtle shades that occurred when the copper first oxidized.

Following the description of the features that apply generally to the entire terminal, it is now time to turn to individual sections and their particular characteristics that existed in the terminal when new.

Approaching the terminal by ferry from Manhattan, there were six arched openings in the waterfront facade, each flanked by wooden racks to form individual docking slips. When the river ran fast past the mouth of the slips, it was virtually impossible for the captain to make a straight shot without touching the racks. They were designed for guidance into the docking position, and they gave when hit head on or with a glancing blow, to soften the impact.

Bells clattered and engines were put into reversing position, sending frothy white water churning ahead beneath the main deck as the ferry snuggled under the toggle beam at the end of the wooden transfer bridge. A floating pontoon kept the height of the transfer bridge even with the ferry's vehicle deck at any stage of the tide, the normal variation between the high and low water being five feet. More modern terminals today use electric motors to raise and lower the bridge to fit the boats.

The passenger aprons for access to the upper deck were rigidly connected to the transfer bridge to maintain the necessary spacing; but they had an overhead device that prevented them from collapsing onto the deck in the event that the ferry crashed into the transfer bridge and forced it backward, severing the apron's connecting supports.

If the contact was particularly severe, the entire building structure would sway and the buffer platform at the land end would absorb some of the impact, after which the transfer bridge would slide across the concourse floor. When the 1891-built steam ferry "Hamburg," later "Chatham," was dieselized and renamed "Lackawanna" in 1949, the boat had a reputation for slamming into the transfer bridges more often than any other ferry because the diesel engines reacted to orders more slowly.

During the rush hour all six slips would be used. In 1907, the most northerly slips, numbers one and two, served West 23rd Street; three and four were for Christopher Street, straight across the river; and five and six, for the busiest route to Barclay Street in Lower Manhattan. At nights and on weekends, only one slip was required for each run and every other slip would be used for lay-up.

The ferries' timing was most important, and if they were on schedule and properly spaced they should not have to wait for a vacant slip. To minimize delays the precise departure times were rigidly observed. For instance, the last Christopher Street ferry for a train departure at 5:10 pm would leave its Manhattan slip

During the approach by ferry from Barclay Street, three of the original five ferries ordered by the Lackawanna occupy half of the six slips. (Conrad Milster)

only ten minutes earlier, at 5:00 pm. Precious minutes could be lost and a train missed, if, for example, a giant Cunarder passing upriver to its Chelsea berth interrupted the ferry's scheduled 7-minute crossing. In later schedules the ferry departed fifteen minutes before train time.

The double-decked ferry fleet built in 1904 and 1905 had certificates for almost 2000 passengers, and two levels in the terminals allowed for rapid loading.

Passengers leaving via the upper deck entered a monumental concourse that stretched for 470 feet along the entire length of the six ferry slips, containing 29,000 square feet of floor space and making it one of the largest unobstructed interior spaces in the world, rivaling the great Hall of Mirrors at Versailles. Massive round columns with ionic capitals gave the illusion of holding up the ceiling punctuated by rectangular skylights. However, they were made of wire mesh

A black and white post card showing the ferryboat Binghamton in the most southerly slip beneath the grand four-faced clock tower at the Lackawanna Terminal. The penny post card was mailed in September 1908 from a woman in Jersey City to a friend in Rhinebeck, New York. (Howard Samelson Collection).

Lackawanna R. R. Terminal from River Hoboken, N. J.

To the left and right of the ferry Pocono, originally Scandinavia, some of the fine details can be seen above the slip openings. The "Lackawanna" letters are six feet high and illuminated at night. (Charles Luffbarry)

Lackawanna Ferry, R. R. Station and Trolley Terminal, Hoboken, N. J.

P-1646

A color post card showing the forecourt of the Lackawanna Terminal with the trolley terminal off to the right. (Howard Samelson Collection).

plaster and were hollow and merely decorative, while the real columns were smaller ones made of steel.

The artificial lighting here did not have the intensity of that in some of the other interior spaces, as the huge room was mostly used as a passageway from the boats to the trains and the street. Arriving ferry passengers heading for their trains could use a wide ramp, lighted by chandeliers, that sloped down towards the train concourse, ending in a flight of stairs just opposite the most northerly set of tracks; or they could choose the pair of stairs that led directly into the main waiting room. The view from the landing overlooking the room could not fail to impress, even today. Passengers wishing to reach the streetcars or Hoboken's business district took the stairs down to the team entrance.

Later, when the Public Service trolley car terminal was added, abutting the railroad Y.M.C.A., itself not a part of the original plan, connecting passengers could walk straight forward along the arcade to the upper level facility.

Passengers leaving the ferries via the main deck could reach their trains by-passing first into the main waiting room through sliding doors beneath the grand staircase, or through the team entrances, then turning

Sam Sloan's association with the D.L.&W. spanned 43 years, first as a director in 1864, then as president from 1867 to 1899, and finally as chairman to his death in 1907. He was the person most responsible for building the Lackawanna into a great eastern passenger and freight carrier. (The author)

34

A view of the ornate exterior of the central waiting room. Note the date 1907 at the top above Lackawanna R. R. September 1980. (The author).

Ornate copper plating covers a steel frame over the entrance to one of the ferry slips at the Hoboken Terminal in September 1980. (The author).

left into the waiting room and out onto the train concourse.

Foot passengers had to use caution when leaving via the lower deck so as not to become entangled with the vehicular traffic exiting the ferry house into the bricked public square. A statue of Sam Sloan, the Lackawanna's president from 1867 to 1899 and chairman of the board to his death in 1907, formed square's the centerpiece.

The five bays in the ferry house facade facing the street have the most elaborate and detailed copper decoration of all, with a rich variety of shapes in which the abstract predominates. Some recognizable sculpture depicts fishes, scallop shells, and stylized plants and flowers.

Large brass letters over the arched windows of the railroad offices announced FERRIES TO NEW YORK, and embedded in the canopy perimeter were the names of the three ferry routes to Manhattan — TWENTY-THIRD STREET, CHRISTOPHER STREET and BARCLAY STREET.

To the right of the bays leading into the ferry house, the ornamental facade of the main waiting room had LACKAWANNA R.R. written proudly at the top up, some 50 feet from the street, and the year 1907 inscribed above that.

Later the Railroad Y.M.C.A. was added, jutting out into the forecourt but maintaining the uniform texture of the entire terminal's facade. The facility provided the railroad's operating crews with inexpensive hotel, eating and recreational facilities. Today, like the ferry house, the facility is entirely abandoned, and while the exterior is kept in repair, the interior is badly decayed.

From a decorative standpoint, the terminal's greatest interior space had to be the main waiting room, with a floor area and ceiling height of generous proportions, roughly a hundred feet square and slightly over fifty feet high.

Illumination came from almost a thousand small lamps, some embedded in the plaster rosettes and others dangling from four huge chandeliers; through large windows facing the ramps to the north and south and through another set of glazed windows bringing in natural light from the west over the train shed. To the east, the windows faced in the direction of the upper ferry concourse. But by far the most spectacular feature was the Tiffany ceiling of colored glass in a geometric design lighted from above by more incandescent lamps.

Some of the colors in the ceiling were repeated in the colored glass signs above the ticket windows and over entrances to the lunch room and restaurant.

To lessen the incidence of cracking, the floor was laid in several layers, first with an inch of dry sand covering the fireproof concrete base. On top of that there was a layer of tarpaper, then 2½ inches of cinder-concrete mix. The terrazzo wearing surface was an inch and a half of concrete into which colored Italian marble chips in different patterns were embedded and then polished smooth. The pleasing effect nicely complements the patches of color found elsewhere in the room.

Ornamental iron was used in the false balconies at the base of the tall windows and, more elaborately, in the stair railings leading from the waiting room floor to the landing at the entrance to the upper ferry concourse.

Buff limestone walls rose up to the base of the windows, then plaster took over from there and continued up and over the elaborate ceiling surrounding the Tiffany skylight. A large clock ringed with a plaster design was set into the west wall.

There were only four ticket windows along the north wall, as most passengers coming from New York had already purchased their through ferry and train tickets at one of several locations in Lower and Mid-Manhattan or at one of the three Manhattan ferry houses. Many of the Lackawanna's patrons were regular commuters, and they bought multiple-ride tickets at their local New Jersey stations. Passengers who arrived at the terminal by means other than the ferries used the ticket facilities.

Doors from the west end of the waiting room led onto the 307-foot train concourse that stretched the length of the iron gates leading to fourteen, later expanded to seventeen, tracks. Skylights of wire mesh glass brought natural light into the space that gave access not only to the trains but to the ramps leading up to the upper ferry concourse, to the baggage room opposite Track 1, to the

Illumination pouring through the Tiffany glass skylight bathes the main waiting room in light prior to the terminal's opening in February 1907. Three of the four chandeliers hang from long chains rooted in the plaster ceiling. In contrast to today's restoration, the iron work lining the base of the windows and the iron staircase are painted a much darker shade. The ornate lighting fixtures have not yet been placed above the settees. Note the "SMOKING ROOM" sign back of the benches, where today's "MEN" is located. Not all the light fixtures are in place. (D.L.&W. photo by W. B. Barry, Jr., John Willever Collection)

street at the north end and to the immigrant slip at the south end.

Barges and ferries from Ellis Island brought the newly-arrived steerage passengers to special trains for the coalfields of northeastern Pennsylvania and further west, bringing substantial business to the Lackawanna Railroad. The simple two-story building at the end of the immigrant slips served partly as a waiting room for these passengers and partly as a Pullman Company facility.

From all accounts the terminal's two famous eating places bring back as many happy memories as do the long-distance trains and the ferries.

In the main waiting room, at the bottom of the stairs on the south wall, blue glass letters read LUNCH ROOM. Inside, the large facility had tables and counter seats and was popular with train and ferry riders in a bit of a hurry and with modest means.

Far more impressive, and of greater interest to New Yorkers and Jerseyites who may have had little or no interest at all in using the trains, was the grand restaurant located at the southeast corner of the terminal building at the far end of the upper ferry concourse.

The main dining room, 72 feet by 53 feet, was described by John Perry in his *American Ferryboats* of

In this photograph taken ten years after the terminal opened, note the "NO EXIT" sign beneath the stairs. Ferry passengers passed through this door into the waiting room but were to use other routes when headed from the trains to the boats. The floor is two shades of terrazzo framed by mosaic. (D.L.&W. photo by John G. Anneman, March 3, 1917, John Willever Collection)

1957 as a "fine restaurant, finished in rare woods, bronze, gilt and gleaming mirrors with white linen on the tables and attentive waiters." Not a great deal has been written about the menu but we do know that the river view was a fine one, and the restaurant had an excellent reputation.

Even in 1907 there was not much of a chance for local residents to reach the river unless they worked there or were taking a boat somewhere, and the Lackawanna Terminal restaurant derived much of its popularity from having windows that faced onto the river. In the summer diners could eat outside on an balcony covered with a broad awning and enjoy the sights, sounds and smells of the river.

From an architectural and functional viewpoint, the train shed, designed by Lincoln Bush, the Chief Engineer for the Lackawanna Railroad from 1902 to 1909, was the most innovative feature of the the entire plan.

Previous to the Bush Train Shed, described shortly, the most common design for very large stations was the wide-span or umbrella or balloon-type shed of which there were many examples in existence at the time. The Pennsylvania Railroad's nearby waterfront terminal at Exchange Place had a notable one, and even better known was Philadelphia's Broad Street Station and the Reading Terminal, the latter the only remaining one in the country today. However, the new Center City Commuter Tunnel, opened for full operations in 1984 to link the Pennsylvania- and Reading-side commuter lines, made the old terminal redundant.

While the umbrella shed was spectacularly spacious, it was costly to build, to maintain and to heat. Steam-era trains vented their smoke upward only to be trapped beneath the roof, on busy days creating an unpleasantly polluted atmosphere.

Lincoln Bush's design used a series of seven low-level canopies, with each one spanning 20-foot platforms serving two tracks. The 607-foot steel and concrete canopies, held up by fluted iron columns topped with ionic capitals supporting transverse-arched plate girders, protected the passengers from the elements while allowing natural light to enter through wire mesh glass skylights.

Open smoke ducts over the center of each track, running the entire length of the shed and just clearing the height of the trains, allowed the steam engines' smoke to escape directly upward into the air and not accumulate under the canopy roof. The passengers breathed cleaner air, the interior of the train shed proved to be cooler on hot days, and there was less heat loss in the winter. In addition, the entire low-level structure was much easier and cheaper to build and maintain.

Except during torrential downpours when water would drop through the narrow openings and cascade

Fluted ionic columns support the flared girders holding up the canopies that span two tracks on each side of central platforms. When the terminal was brand-new, the skylights allowed lots of natural light into the train shed. In the second picture engine #952 emits its smoke through the narrow slits that run the full length of the train shed. The type of opaque glass seen in this latter shot is more durable but allows less light to reach the platforms. (Both photos D.L.&W. by W. B. Barry, Jr., Homer Hill Collection)

The Pennsylvania Railroad's 19th century terminal at Exchange Place in Jersey City was one of the best examples of an umbrella type train shed, a glass and steel structure overing the tracks and platforms. Before Penn Station, New York was completed in 1910, the PRR's terminal was the most important on the North River waterfront and its ferries comprised the largest fleet. (William H. Ewen, Jr. Collection)

Pennsylvania Railroad Depot.   Jersey City, N. J.

from the roof of the passenger coaches, most of the rain accumulated in the canopies' gutters and was carried by pipes through the center of the hollow columns into the drains beneath the platforms.

The entire shed covered almost five acres, and beyond the end of each row of ornamental columns, a decorative lamp stood on a roof pedestal above the carved initials 'D.L.&W.' facing west.

The platforms extended another 100 feet beyond the end of the shed, alongside of which engines of particularly long trains stood.

The sum total of all these parts was a unique railroad and ferry terminal of tremendous importance; and when the Lackawanna facility opened to the public at 6:00 am on the morning of February 25, 1907, it was deservedly heralded as the finest waterfront transportation complex in the world.

Beyond the train shed, Engine #982, a 4-4-0, rests on the turntable outside the roundhouse, while further west, two lines of fully-coaled locomotives wait on the ready track. (Both photos D.L.&W. by W. B. Barry, Jr., John Willever Collection)

This architectural rendering by Kenneth Murchison shows the fine detail of the West 23rd Street Terminal's front elevation. Note the several cartouches showing 'LACKAWANNA RAILROAD', the initials 'LR' and the anchor. It is interesting to compare this drawing with the actual terminal when completed. (Museum of the City of New York) **The important West 23rd Street ferry terminal had many of the same characteristics as the Lackawanna Terminal in Hoboken, a highly decorative pile of copper sheathing over a steel frame. Besides serving the Lackawanna ferries, there were boats to the Central of New Jersey Terminal and, out of sight, to the Erie's Pavonia terminal, both located on the waterfront in Jersey City. The 14th Street crosstown streetcar gets its power from a source beneath the street rather than from overhead wires. West 23rd Street declined in importance over the years as midtown Manhattan moved north, and because the ferry terminal was not directly linked with the subway and elevated rapid transit lines.** (Berenice Abbott, Museum of the City of New York)

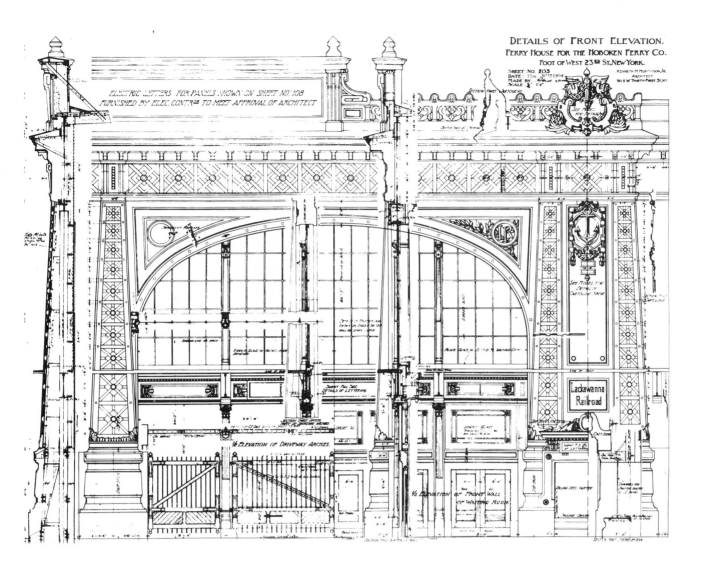

DETAILS OF FRONT ELEVATION.
FERRY HOUSE FOR THE HOBOKEN FERRY CO.
FOOT OF WEST 23RD ST. NEW YORK.

CHAPTER III
LACKAWANNA TRAINS FROM 1907

When the Hoboken Terminal opened for business in February 1907, travelers could buy tickets for a ride of 14 miles to the end of the Montclair Branch or 396 miles along the main line to the very end of the property at Buffalo. Milepost "Zero" began at the Lackawanna's Barclay Street, Christopher Street and West 23rd Street ferry terminals in Manhattan, while Hoboken itself, the beginning of the railway, was designated Mile 1.0.

Between these extremes passengers could travel on the Morris and Essex Division for 85 miles through the Oranges and Summit to Morristown, Hackettstown, and Phillipsburg and Easton, the latter two on opposite sides of the Delaware River. Leaving the M & E at Summit, through trains ran over the Passaic and Delaware to Far Hills and Gladstone, 42 miles from Hoboken. Additional local service based in Hoboken ran through Boonton, on the Chester Branch and on the Sussex Branch to Franklin and Branchville.

Over the main line, Lackawanna long-distance trains traveled the Bloomsburg Division to Northumberland in northeastern Pennsylvania, and to Utica and Richfield Springs on the Utica Division, to Oswego on Lake Ontario and on short branches to Ithaca, Montrose and Cincinnatus, all in New York State.

Of all the fine trains that the D.L.&W. operated, the flagship of the fleet was the "Lackawanna Limited," scheduled for a fast daylight run from Hoboken to Buffalo with a through sleeping car over the Nickel Plate to

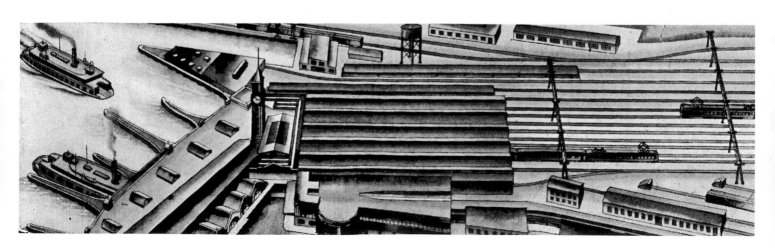

Chicago. Launched in 1899 when William H. Truesdale replaced Sam Sloan as D.L.&W. president, the "Lackawanna Limited" would remain in the timetables for half a century, until the premier train switched from steam to diesel power in November 1949.

The train that would take the place of the "Lackawanna Limited" was the "Phoebe Snow," a well-known name first used in 1904 as one of the railroad industry's most successful advertising campaigns.

To publicize the D.L.&W.'s use of clean-burning anthracite coal to fire its steam locomotive fleet, the railroad's advertising department came up with a mythical maiden named Phoebe Snow who rode the trains clothed in a white dress, floppy hat and gloves. On her travels not a bit of coal dust smudged her pristine garments. Throughout her long career, interrupted during the First World War when the U.S. Government requisitioned the Lackawanna's anthracite for use in ships at sea, no less than 69 3- to 8-line poems were penned to caption the railroad's ad campaign. While some of the verse was rather obscure and not very good poetry, this popular four-liner reveals the spirit intended:

> Her laundry bill for fluff and frill
> Miss Phoebe finds is nearly nil.
> It's always light though gowns of white
> are worn on Road of Anthracite.

In this publicity shot, an advance section of the "Lackawanna Limited," indicated by the green flags at the front of the Pacific-type 4-6-2, poses on the four-track main line at Mile 124 about ten miles east of Scranton in about 1912. (Gouldsboro & Lehigh, John Willever Collection)

Another ditty that does not appear in the Lackawanna's official records, but whose message may be closer to the truth in the pre-air-conditioned days of open-window steam trains, goes like this:

> Said Phoebe Snow in the dining car,
> "I did not order caviar."
> The waiter dusted off the bread,
> "This is not caviar," he said.

On the Lackawanna main line to Buffalo, a far more important passenger destination that it is today, the railroad, with the shortest route, competed with the New York Central, the Erie, the Lehigh Valley and the Pennsylvania for the fastest running times and the best service.

In *The Official Guide of the Railways* of January 1930, the largest edition ever published with 1800 pages of train schedules and information, the New York Central's "Empire State Express" comes out on top with an end-to-end time of 9 hours, 10 minutes over its 436-mile route, 15 minutes faster than the D.L.&W.'s "Lackawanna Limited" running over 395 miles. Both trains carried observation parlor cars and dining cars to capture the top end of the market. The New York Central's Water Level Route followed the Hudson and Mohawk Valleys, allowing for much higher speeds than the twisting Lackawanna route through the Pocono Mountains. The Central had as many as seven daytime departures from Grand Central to Buffalo as opposed to the D.L.&W.'s one, and that train left from Hoboken.

By June 1941 the "Empire State Express" broke the eight-hour mark by five minutes, and after that there was really no contest when it came to speed.

Almost one hundred car repairmen pose in front, with one on the roof, of a D.L.&W. reefer car in about 1901. (Joel Lipman Collection) **Many railroads advertised their name trains on the sides of the freight cars. Here two box cars on a local freight proudly announce "Lackawanna The Route of Phoebe Snow" at Morristown in the early 1950's.** (Homer R. Hill) **The Lackawanna tug Utica powers a car float down the East River having just passed beneath the Brooklyn Bridge, en route most likely from the Lackawanna's Harlem Transfer in the Bronx to Hoboken, in the 1940's. The D.L.&W. had its own car float operations numerous waterfront sites in Brooklyn, the Bronx and along the East and North Rivers.** (George Swede, Steamship Historical Society)

Streamliner Pacific #1117, 4-6-2, built in 1922 in front of the coal docks. (Joel Lipman Collection)

An inkblotter from the 1920's advertises the three Lackawanna trains from Syracuse, joining the main line at Binghamton. Passengers had a convenient choice of early morning, midday and overnight departures for New York or Philadelphia. Note that the Lackawanna is recommending the Hudson Tube for the New York connection rather than its own ferries. (Joel Lipman Collection)

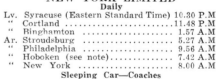
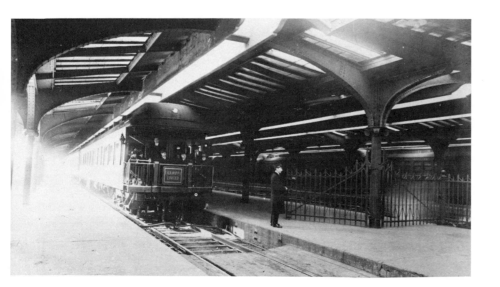

The gateman is about to close out the morning departure of the "Lackawanna Limited" from Track 15 as passengers crowd the observation car's open platform. The train's route passes through the Poconos along the Southern Tier in New York State to Buffalo, where a portion of the train will continue via the Nickel Plate to Chicago. (D.L.&W. photo by W. B. Barry, Jr., Homer Hill Collection)

The Erie Railroad's parlor and dining car equipped "Erie Limited" covered its 424-mile route between Jersey City and Buffalo in 10 hours, 20 minutes while the Lehigh Valley sent the "Black Diamond" from Penn Station over 447 miles in 11 hours, 8 minutes. The Lehigh Valley's train featured an observation lounge sunroom, parlor car with drawing rooms, and stock market reports, no doubt a service of some interest during the first months following the Great Crash on Wall Street.

The Pennsylvania's 506-mile route, taking over 12 hours, was not much of a contender in this day train market.

In the lucrative overnight business trade, where convenient departure and arrival schedules were even more important than speed, all five railroads sent out sleeping car trains offering club lounges and dining service.

On the longer through route to Chicago, the Lackawanna could not compete at all, and really did not try, with the Pennsylvania's crack "Broadway Limited" and the Central's classy "Twentieth Century Limited."

Buffalo, at the far end of the Lackawanna property, received a new Lake Erie waterfront terminal in 1917 where passengers and freight could directly transfer to and from Great Lakes' steamers bound for ports in Lakes Huron, Michigan and Superior. The white-hulled vessel at the right is the Fort Huron-registered Northland or Southland. (D.L.&W. photo by W. B. Barry, Jr., John Willever Collection)

In this publicity photograph, dated January 31, 1928, engineer Benjamin Locke makes his last run before retirement, taking a Pacific-type locomotive over the old main line to Stroudsburg. The crowd to the left is paying tribute to 53 years of service and a perfect safety record. As part of Lackawanna tradition, every engine sounds its whistle when an operating employee retires, to this very day. (D.L.&W. photo by W. B. Barry, Jr., John Willever Collection)

This pair of early photographs was taken in 1913 just prior to Morristown Line track elevation that would eventually extend from Newark to Convent Station. Looking down the tracks towards the station at Orange, note the horizontal device under the trolley wire to protect it from the heavy exhaust of steam locomotives. Further out is the Waverly Place level crossing adjacent to the Madison station in the heart of that town's business district. (Both photos - D.L.&W. by W. B. Barry, Jr., John Willever Collection)

A passenger extra, flying two white flags, waits in the hole at the far end of the station at Dover, the end of today's Morristown Line suburban service, on July 28, 1911. To the right of the water plug, removed at the end of steam locomotive operations in June 1953, stands a call boy holding a hoop for getting train orders on the fly. (D.L.&W. photo by W. B. Barry, Jr., John Willever Collection)

The Lackawanna's main markets were the intermediate stops on the route through the Pocono resorts, Scranton and the Southern Tier in New York State; where the D.L.&W.'s "Chicago Limited," "Western Special," "Whitelight Limited" and "Buffalo Mail" were pitted against the Erie's "Chicago Express," "Lake Cities Express" and "Pacific Express." Here the Lackawanna had good reason to be proud of its trains, and they were very popular with the traveling public.

Under the leadership of Lackawanna President John M. Davis, who followed William H. Truesdale, the railroad completed a suburban electrification program that rivaled the Pennsylvania's significant improvements to its New York-Washington line and the local Pennsy and Reading electrified services out of Philadelphia.

Smoke and cinders from steam locomotives, the delight of most railfans today, were exceedingly unpopular with suburban residents who lived along lines with

Restored D.L.&W. #952, 4-4-0, exhibited at the New York World's Fair in 1939, is seen at Hoboken in the same year. Above the unidentified man at the right is a Boonton Line club car. (R. A. Le Massena) **Boxcab #3001, the D.L.&W.'s first diesel, built in 1926, is switching a Boonton Line coach at Hoboken in the late 1940's with the Lackawanna freight house in the background.** (Jon Franz Collection) **The westbound "Lackawanna Limited," headed by #1404, a 4-8-2, races through Morristown in the early 1940's.** (Homer R. Hill)

Thomas A. Edison (foreground, center) inaugurates electrified service on the Lackawanna Railroad on September 3, 1930 from Hoboken Terminal. (NJ Transit).

THOMAS A. EDISON ACTS AS ENGINEER

'Phoebe Snow' Among Big, Happy Throng Riding Lackawanna's New Iron Horse from South Orange to Hoboken

PASSENGERS THRILLED OVER TRIP

Cheers and Waves Greet 800 First Riders All Along Road—Railroad Officials Among Those Making Journey

Thomas A. Edison started the first electric passenger train through the Oranges this morning, when he pressed the controller of a 10-car train at 9:44 starting the train from South Orange.

Mrs. Edison was at the controls too and "Phoebe Snow" had a hand in the proceedings.

William J. Orchard, president of the Chamber of

Commerce and Civics, a prime mover in the fight for electrification and many others also operated the train.

Crowds along the route of the train to Newark cheered as the electric train passed through. Hundreds aboard the train were thrilled, as the start was made—forecasting the eventual elimination of smoke and soot through the territory covered by the Lackawanna Railroad.

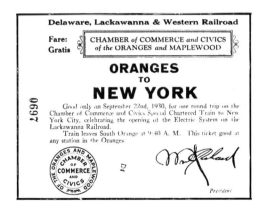

A souvenir ticket that gives one passenger a free ride on the inaugural train from South Orange at 9:40 a.m. on September 22, 1930. The accompanying article indicates that the train actually left four minutes late at 9:44 a.m. (Howard Samelson Collection).

frequent services and with city dwellers in the neighborhood of the Hoboken Terminal yards. But with the commuter business growing fast, the railroad needed to be able to increase capacity as well as improve service to this important market.

Thomas Alva Edison was reported to have been at the controls of the very first electric train out of Hoboken on September 3, 1930, en route to Montclair. By January 25, 1931, some 68 miles had come under the wires, including the Morristown Line to Dover, the Gladstone Branch and the already mentioned Montclair Branch. With much faster acceleration now possible, the reduction in running times averaged about 20 percent; and by the beginning of 1931, some 300 new electric trains were arriving and departing Hoboken on an average weekday.

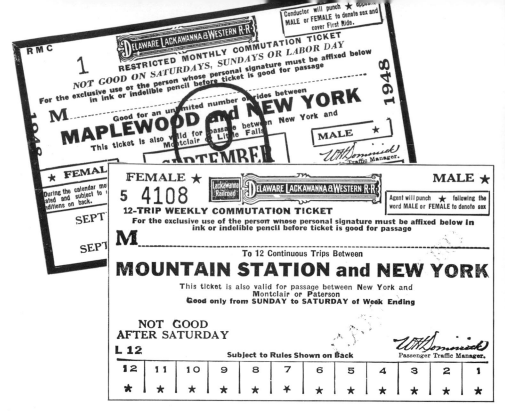

A restricted monthly commutation ticket from September 1948 between Maplewood and New York and another 12-trip weekly ticket for the week prior to Christmas 1954 for travel between Mountain Station and New York. Users of these two tickets had the ferry fare included. The signature of W. H. Dominick, Passenger Traffic Manager, appeared on hundreds of thousands of Lackawanna tickets in the 1940's and 1950's. (Joel Lipman Collection)

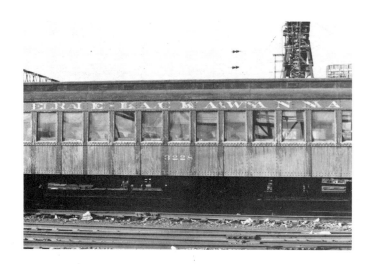

On the side of trailer car 3228, built in 1925, the old letters 'Lackawanna' are showing through the much newer addition 'Erie-Lackawanna'. Electric 3541, built in 1930, looks much neater, though without the hyphen separating the names (Both photos - the author) 'Erie-Lackawanna' appeared above the three ticket windows at the time of merger in 1960. Blue stained glass letters adorn the openings in the limestone facade. (The author)

This pair of MU's seen at Gladstone in July, 1970, formed a small part of a once great fleet of "Morristown Electrics" that faithfully served New Jersey commuters for over 25 years. Some cars even pre-dated electrification in 1930, and dated back to 1917 and earlier. (David Hill) Dover Towers, at the end of the electrified Morristown Line, sits across the road from the yard and station which is now an historic landmark. (Fielding L. Bowman) A midday line-up of commuter power stands ready in Hoboken, also in the summer of 1970. (Howard Pincus)

Lackawanna Railroad — The Route of Phoebe Snow

CONDENSED EQUIPMENT OF TRAINS—PARLOR AND SLEEPING CAR LINES, DINING CAR SERVICE—REGULARLY ASSIGNED CARS ARE AIR-CONDITIONED

WESTWARD

THE PHOEBE SNOW No. 3—DAILY
De luxe Streamliner
(Via Nickel Plate No. 5)

SLEEPING CAR
New York to Chicago
(10 Roomettes—6 Double Bedrooms) (Car 30)
OBSERVATION LOUNGE CAR (D. L. & W.)
New York to Buffalo (Open to all passengers)
DINING CAR
New York to Buffalo
CLUB-DINER-LOUNGE CAR
Buffalo to Chicago
RECLINING SEAT COACHES
New York to Chicago
New York to Buffalo
Binghamton to Syracuse

THE TWILIGHT No. 5
DAILY EXCEPT SATURDAY
(Via New York Central No. 47-375)
(Saturday Equipment is operated in Train
No. 25, except Sleeping and Parlor Cars)

SLEEPING CAR
New York to Detroit (Daily except Saturday)
(6 Sec.—6 Double Bedrooms) (Car 50)
BUFFET LOUNGE CAR SERVICE
New York to Binghamton
PARLOR CAR (D. L. & W.)
New York to Corning (Daily except Saturday)
(Drawing Room) (Car 51)
DINING CAR
New York to Binghamton
Detroit to Chicago
RECLINING SEAT COACHES
New York to Buffalo
Detroit to Chicago

THE WESTERNER No. 7—DAILY
(Via Nickel Plate No. 7)

SLEEPING CARS
New York to Chicago
(10 Roomettes—6 Double Bedrooms) (Car 70)
New York to Buffalo
(10 Roomettes—6 Double Bedrooms) (Car 71)—
May be occupied until 7.00 A.M.
BUFFET LOUNGE CAR
New York to Scranton
DINER LOUNGE CAR
Buffalo to Chicago
RECLINING SEAT COACHES
New York to Chicago
New York to Buffalo
Buffalo to Chicago

THE OWL No. 15—DAILY

SLEEPING CARS
New York to Elmira (Daily except Friday night)
(10 Roomettes—6 Double Bedrooms) (Car 150)
New York to Buffalo (Friday night only)
(10 Roomettes—6 Double Bedrooms) (Car 150)
New York to Syracuse (Daily except Saturday night)
(10 Sec.—D.R.—2 Double Bedrooms) (Car 152)—
In No. 1915 from Binghamton
New York to Binghamton (Daily except Saturday night)
(10 Roomettes—6 Double Bedrooms) (Car 151)—
May be occupied until 7.00 A.M.
Sleeping cars open for occupancy at Hoboken 8.30 P.M.
DINER LOUNGE CAR
Binghamton to Buffalo
Binghamton to Syracuse
RECLINING SEAT COACHES
New York to Buffalo
Binghamton to Syracuse

WESTWARD

INTERSTATE EXPRESS No. 1301—DAILY
(Via B. & O. Reading Co. and C.R.R. of N. J.)

SLEEPING CAR
Philadelphia to Syracuse
(8 Sec.—5 Single Bedrooms) (Car 301)—
In No. 1915 from Binghamton—
Open for occupancy at 9.00 P.M.
PARLOR-DINING-LOUNGE CAR
Washington to Philadelphia, via B. & O. R.R.
DINER LOUNGE CAR
Binghamton to Syracuse
Binghamton to Buffalo
RECLINING SEAT COACHES
Washington to Philadelphia
In B. & O. No. 36 from Washington
COACHES
Philadelphia to Wilkes-Barre
In Reading Co. No. 301 from Philadelphia; non air-
conditioned
RECLINING SEAT COACHES
Binghamton to Syracuse
Binghamton to Buffalo

EASTWARD

POCONO EXPRESS No. 2
DAILY EXCEPT SUNDAY AND HOLIDAYS
(Sunday and Holidays Equipment is operated
in Train No. 4.)

SLEEPING CAR
Detroit to New York (Daily except Saturday)
(6 Sec. — 6 Double Bedrooms) (Car 440) via New
York Central No. 44.
SLEEPING CAR
Buffalo to New York
(6 Sec. — 6 Double Bedrooms) (Car 440) (Daily
except Sat. night-Sun. morning) from N. Y. C. No. 44.
Buffalo to New York
(10 Roomettes—6 Double Bedrooms) (Car 20)
(Saturday night-Sunday morning only)
Cars may be occupied at Buffalo at 11.00 P.M.
DINING CAR
Elmira to New York
RECLINING SEAT COACHES
Buffalo to New York

THE PHOEBE SNOW No. 6—DAILY
De luxe Streamliner

OBSERVATION LOUNGE CAR (D. L. & W.)
Buffalo to New York
(Open to all passengers)
PARLOR CAR (D. L. & W.)
Buffalo to New York (Daily except Saturday)
(Drawing Room) (Car 61)
DINING CAR
Buffalo to New York
BUFFET LOUNGE CAR
Syracuse to Binghamton
RECLINING SEAT COACHES
Buffalo to New York
Syracuse to Binghamton

EASTWARD

THE NEW YORKER No. 8—DAILY
(Via Nickel Plate No. 8)

SLEEPING CARS
Chicago to New York
(10 Roomettes—6 Double Bedrooms) (Car 80)
Buffalo to New York
(10 Roomettes—6 Double Bedrooms) (Car 83)—
Open for occupancy at 8.00 P.M.
Elmira to New York (Daily except Saturday night)
(10 Roomettes—6 Double Bedrooms) (Car 84)
Open for occupancy at 8.30 P.M.
Sleeping cars may be occupied at Hoboken until 7.00 A.M.
DINER LOUNGE CAR
Chicago to Buffalo
RECLINING SEAT COACHES
Chicago to New York
Buffalo to New York

NEW YORK MAIL No. 10—DAILY
(Via Nickel Plate No. 6)

SLEEPING CARS
Chicago to New York
(10 Roomettes—6 Double Bedrooms) (Car 60)
Syracuse to New York (Daily except Saturday night)
(10 Sec.—D.R.—2 Double Bedrooms) (Car 101)—
In No. 1910 to Binghamton.
Binghamton to New York (Daily except Saturday night)
(10 Roomettes—6 Double Bedrooms) (Car 100)
Open for occupancy at 8.30 P.M.
Sleeping cars may be occupied at Hoboken until 7.00 A.M.
CLUB-DINER-LOUNGE CAR
Chicago to Buffalo
BUFFET LOUNGE CAR
Buffalo to Elmira
RECLINING SEAT COACHES
Chicago to Buffalo
Buffalo to New York
Syracuse to Binghamton

MERCHANTS EXPRESS No. 26
DAILY EXCEPT SUNDAY AND HOLIDAYS

DINER LOUNGE CAR
Scranton to New York
RECLINING SEAT COACHES
Scranton to New York

INTERSTATE EXPRESS No. 1306—DAILY
(Via C.R.R. of N. J. No. 306—Reading Co. No. 306-2306)

SLEEPING CAR
Syracuse to Philadelphia
(8 Sec.—5 Single Bedrooms) (Car 130)—
In No. 1910 from Syracuse
COACHES
Wilkes-Barre to Philadelphia
In C.R.R. of N. J. No. 306 from Wilkes-Barre;
non air-conditioned
RECLINING SEAT COACHES
Syracuse to Binghamton
Buffalo to Binghamton

No. 44-46—DAILY

BUFFET LOUNGE CAR
Binghamton to New York
RECLINING SEAT COACHES
Binghamton to New York

This panel from a Lackawanna timetable dated July 24, 1954 showed a prospective passenger everything he needed to know about what a train would offer on a westward journey. The four major name trains gave convenient departures spread throughout the day, with equally spaced arrival times at stations all along the 395-mile train line. Every train carried a diner or diner lounge and sleeping cars, where if parlor service was not available, then passengers could book day seats in roomettes or bedrooms for a small extra charge. A roomette overnight to Buffalo cost $24.84 and the same accommodation to Chicago via the Nickel Plate cost $51.39. There were generous reductions for the round-trip rail fare that would bring down the one-way rates even further. (Robert C. Lake Collection)

The steam era is just about to expire on the Lackawanna. A three-coach, two-milk car Branchville Local accelerates way from Netcong, and a much longer Branchville train, also carrying two milk cars from Hoboken, heads westward under the wires between Denville and Dover, in February and May 1953. (Both photos by Homer R. Hill)

A brakeman on the rear platform of an open vestibule mail and baggage combine watches 4-year-old David Hill, son of the photographer, pace the Hoboken-bound Boonton Branch local in February 1953. (Homer R. Hill)

On November 10, 1961, a westbound Gladstone Branch train with failed brakes went off the end of the line and slammed into this house, and though its occupants were home, no one was injured. The trailer car, built by Pullman in 1917, already had its seats walked-over for the trip back to Hoboken. (David Hill, age 13)

The "Phoebe Snow" appeared in 1949 as the Lackawanna's premier train on a daylight run to Buffalo with through coaches and a sleeping car to Chicago's La Salle Street Station. When the traffic warranted, the Lackawanna used extra heavyweight cars bought from the Pullman Company as seen here in the early 1950's at Morristown. Unlike the three cars ahead, Poplar Tree is still Pullman-owned. Normally, the train finished with one of its Budd-built flat-end tavern lounge cars as shown in this well-known photo of the "Phoebe Snow" passing eastbound through Morristown. The author returning from a weekend in the Poconos boarded the train at Cresco just after 4 pm enjoying a drink in the observation car and an early dinner. The round-trip fare, with a four-day limit, remained at $6.35 for years, cheaper than the bus, and oh what a difference. (Both photos - Homer R. Hill)

The original 1930 3000-volt DC system and the first-generation electric cars and rebuilt steam-hauled trailer cars, dating from 1917 and 1925, provided excellent service far longer than anyone anticipated. 54 years later the last units of a tired fleet were put out to pasture.

After the war, while suburban ridership continued to grow, though with increasingly higher costs, the long-distance trains had a brief heyday before going into an irreversible decline. Vacationers began to drive to the Poconos and business travelers took to the air for trips to Buffalo and Chicago. Buses, serving more places with greater route flexibility and lower costs, took away some additional traffic.

Consolidation of passenger schedules progressed with painful regularity, and with each new timetable issued, more blank columns appeared. By 1956 the Erie's Pavonia passenger station in Jersey City was in such sorry shape that on October 13th of that year, all non-rush hour and long-distance trains moved less than a mile north to Hoboken. Within two years all remaining passenger business shifted over, and by October 17, 1960, the two railroads merged completely to become the Erie-Lackawanna Railroad, with headquarters in

The track diagram shows the terminal's layout in 1928 when the three ferry services were still running, and the Lackawanna had a healthy freight and passenger business. While most people generally think of the Lackawanna Terminal being only in Hoboken, most of the freight side and part of the passenger yards are in fact within the limits of Jersey City.

Cleveland. Trucks on the new subsidized interstate highway system were killing the railroads' business. Stringent federal regulations did not help either, and rail lines all over the East were beginning a period of serious financial decline that would end in bankruptcy for at least six of them, including the Erie-Lackawanna.

Long-distance trains were further rationalized at the Hoboken Terminal, while on the suburban side, Hoboken handled additional diesel commuter service on the former Erie lines to Ridgewood, Waldwick, Suffern, Port Jervis, Essex Falls, Wanaque-Midvale, Nyack and Spring Valley.

While much of the suburban service remained, all long-distance trains finally got the axe. The "Phoebe Snow" departed for the last time on November 27, 1966, and the "Lake Cities," a former Erie name train, closed out the very last non-suburban service on January 5, 1970. Now there were no trains west of Dover on the Morristown Line, west of Netcong on the Boonton Line or west of Port Jervis on the main line. The mail and express contracts had expired, and the light passenger loads made the long-distance trains big money losers.

With the passing of the last overnight train went the "Snooze Special," a service where coach passengers, for 50 cents, could buy a pillow for the night and then take it home as a memento of the trip, one of the very last trademarks of "The Friendly Service Route."

Says Phoebe Snow who cannot go
Upon her trip to Buffalo.
With my trains now departed and gone,
What more can I say but — so long.

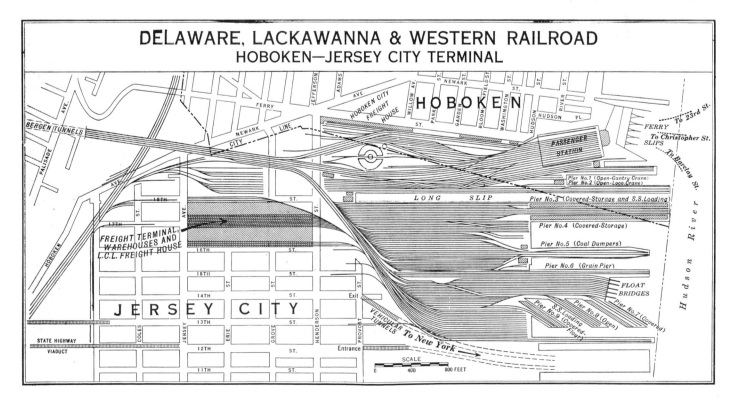

CHAPTER IV
LACKAWANNA FERRIES FROM 1900

The turn of the century was a prosperous time for the Lackawanna Railroad. The brand-new railroad terminal and ferry house in Hoboken, the grand replacement for the ferry house at West 23rd Street, the start up of the "Lackawanna Limited" and the innovative Phoebe Snow campaign reflected the company's sound financial condition.

To complete its control over all operations vital to the movement of passengers and freight, the D.L.&W. acquired in April 1903 the entire stock of the New York and Hoboken Ferry Company from the Eldridge family, who five years before had replaced Stevens family ownership dating almost continuously back to the late 18th Century.

At the time of takeover, the aging ferry fleet was operating at capacity during the rush hours, and new tonnage was desperately needed to alleviate the shortage and improve service. The ferries handled in excess of 100,000 passengers a day on three routes out of the Lackawanna Terminal to Barclay Street, Christopher Street and West 23rd Street, and from 14th Street Hoboken to West 23rd Street Manhattan. The 23rd Street site replaced 14th Street in November 1904.

The Lackawanna placed an order with Newport News Shipbuilding and Drydock Company for five new double-ended, two-deck, 13-miles-per-hour, screw propellor ferryboats costing $211,478.85 each. The boats were 187 feet long, with 986 seats

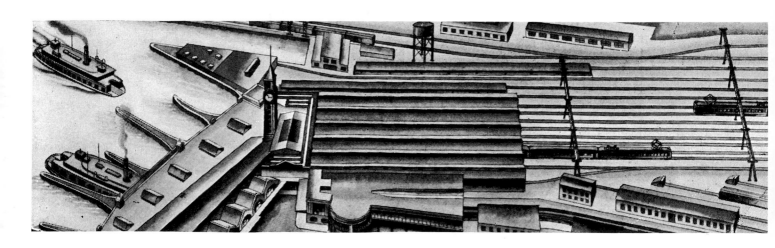

and a passenger certificate for 1986. The vehicle deck, using today's measurements, could handle 14 automobiles. A curious 1908 rule, however, allowed only four cars per trip, two placed forward and two aft, so positioned to be easily pushed overboard in the case of an auto catching fire. The company's books carried this safety regulation long after the practice ceased.

The five new ferries and the rest of the white fleet rose to the height of their popularity, and after the 1910 opening of the Pennsylvania Railroad tunnels into Manhattan, the Lackawanna ferries constituted the largest fleet in the harbor.

During World War I, Hoboken's waterfront piers served as the port of embarkation for American soldiers sailing off to Europe. Between June 1917 and December 1921, over three million troops arrived and left by ship; and more than a million traveled across the river on the Lackawanna ferries, which had passed under government control during the height of the war effort.

Anti-German feeling ran high throughout the country; and the Lackawanna, under pressure in 1918, renamed its ferryboats "Hamburg" and "Bremen," "Chatham" and "Maplewood" respectively. These two minor events occurred about the same time dachshunds became liberty pups and sauerkraut was called liberty cabbage.

In the early 1920's passenger traffic across the Hudson to Manhattan south of 59th Street was evenly divided between the railroad ferries and the Hudson and Manhattan Railroad, each carrying just fewer than 150,000 riders on a typical business day. In addition,

The trim, white Scandinavia completed in 1905, one of the five brand-new ferryboats ordered by the Lackawanna, proudly displays its name and owner in bold two-dimensional lettering in about 1908. The liner in the background would be Cunard's Caronia or Carmania, also new in 1905. (D.L.&W. photo by W. B. Barry, Jr., John Willever Collection) **The sidewheeler Montclair of 1886, rebuilt in 1907 with a second deck hiding the original walking beam, became a regular Christopher Street ferry, until withdrawn in 1942 and sold in 1944 to be used as office space at Rondout, New York. Note the reverse sheer, a prominent feature of the walking beam sidewheeler.** (R. Loren Graham Collection, Steamship Historical Society)

The Barclay Street Ferry dates from 1818 while the building seen here served from 1888 until the ferry closed in 1967. Note the large percentage of trucks and teams, rather than private automobile traffic, lined up for boarding. The vehicles to the left are cabs awaiting foot passengers from Hoboken. Congestion at the piers was a daily occurrence. The walkway crossing West Street led to the Pennsylvania Railroad ferries that ran to Exchange Place in Jersey City. Next door is the New York Central's West Shore Line ferry for Weehawken and north are the piers for the Starin New Haven Line, the D.L.&W. and the Fall River Line to Boston, with the **Priscilla** of 1894 facing outward. (Photo - D.L.&W. by W. B. Barry, Jr., Homer Hill Collection; Post card - author's collection)

The West Street and North River Piers, New York City.

SOUVENIR POST CARD CO., NEW YORK.

6213—BARCLAY STREET FERRY ENTRANCE, HOBOKEN, N. J.

A black and white post card showing the Barclay Street ferry entrance in the old Hoboken Terminal. The postmark dated October 24, 1905 indicates that the card was sent from one New Hampshire address to another over two months after this terminal burned to the ground.
(Howard Samelson Collection)

A sample employee ferry pass from the first quarter of 1922 and a courtesy pass for the employee of another railroad from 1923. (Joel Lipman Collection)

nearly 18,000 passengers a day arrived at Pennsylvania Station from New Jersey.

The five railroads — the Central of New Jersey, Pennsylvania, Erie, Lackawanna and New York Central's West Shore Line — together operated 50 boats on 13 routes. The Lackawanna had the largest passenger traffic, and the Pennsylvania, with good road connections, carried the most heavy-road vehicles.

The results of a regional survey in 1924 found the ferry services adequate for the present and future transportation of foot passengers, but they lacked the capacity to efficiently handle even the current vehicle traffic.

The increasing volume of motor vehicles headed to and from Manhattan caused daily tie-ups at the major ferry terminals. These tie-ups gave impetus to the construction of the Holland and Lincoln Tunnels and the George Washington Bridge.

On the Lackawanna ferry routes, Barclay Street in Lower Manhattan handled almost half the 91,000 daily riders in 1920, while the other three ferry routes equally divided the rest. Vehicular traffic was spread fairly evenly over all four routes, with the 14th Street Ferry slightly exceeding the others, though it was protected by only two boats, while Christopher Street and 23rd Street

The Pennsylvania Railroad's Pittsburgh (1896), after the completion of Pennsylvania Station in 1910, had the vehicle decks widened and carried mostly commercial trucks between Exchange Place and Cortlandt Street. (Charles Luffbarry) Steam tugs, white excursion vessels and the Erie Railroad ferry Tuxedo (1904) shuttling between Pavonia and Chambers Street, fittingly greets the Cunarder Queen Mary on her maiden voyage in 1935. (Fred Sommers) The Central Railroad of New Jersey's Jersey City Terminal with the ferries Somerville (1905) and Elizabeth (1904) served Liberty Street. (Charles Luffbarry) The New York Central's West Shore Line brought train passengers down the Hudson to Weehawken where they transferred to ferries for West 42nd Street and Cortlandt Street in Lower Manhattan. In the center slip is Niagara (1912). (Charles Luffbarry)

The Oswego, originally the Netherlands of 1893, had her upper deck extended to allow for loading on both levels at the new Lackawanna Terminal. Note 'WOMEN' and 'MEN' over the arches at the end of the boat, designating separate cabins on the main deck. The interior was done in Old Colonial style and featured fluted columns. Before the tunnels and bridges took away a lot of the traffic, many trucking firms used the ferries to bring produce and other consumer goods to the New York market. To the right, the Erie ferry Tuxedo is passing. (Capt. Parslow, Steamship Historical Society)

The single-deck ferry Hoboken, with a capacity of 45 cars, was one of the last two ferries built for the Lackawanna in 1922. She made the last run from 14th Street Hoboken in 1942, before transfering to the Christopher treet Ferry until that closed down in 1955. The boat was scrapped in 1957. (Capt. Parslow, Steamship Historical Society) Ferryboat Hoboken's sister Buffalo made the very final Christopher Street run. In the center, the ferryboat Ithaca, one of the five original Lackawanna ferries built between 1904 and 1906, lies gutted by fire in West Brighton, Staten Island in 1946. Over half of the wooden superstructure and the near pilot house were completely destroyed. (Tracey I. Brooks Collection, Steamship Historical Society)

each had three boats assigned and Barclay Street had four. One of the 14th Street Ferry's largest customers was New York City refuse trucks carrying garbage and trash to dump sites in the New Jersey meadowlands.

The 1920's became the turning point for ferry operations, but not all signs were yet understood by the owners and planners. In 1922 the Hoboken Ferry Company launched its last two boats, fittingly called the "Hoboken" and "Buffalo," the two cities being the terminal stations of the Lackawanna's main line.

The only Hudson River railroad ferry built after 1925 was the Erie's "Meadville," completed in 1936 and

licensed to carry 2025 passengers and 26 cars. Ferryboat design had not progressed much; and this boat looked similar to those built before the turn of the century, except for interior decor which was decidedly contemporary.

On November 12, 1927, the Holland Tunnel opened; and almost immediately the number of vehicles on the Lackawanna ferries dropped 30 to 40 per cent. It is generally believed that new roads generate entirely new traffic, and by 1930 the ferry had recovered most of its losses.

Harry J. Smith, at the end of his 1931 book *Romance of the Hoboken Ferry,* made mention of the above and

included some figures to justify his high optimism in the ferry business. "Today," he wrote, "the ferries make a total of 810 trips every 24 hours, annually carrying 25,000,000 passengers and 2,933,000 vehicles."

Then his final paragraph came to this conclusion: "While it is true that ferryboats have been superseded in many sections of the United States by bridges and tunnels, the growth of vehicle and passenger traffic in the metropolitan district of New York is so rapid that possibly another hundred years will elapse before this system of transportation is abandoned."

Unfortunately, the end for the Hudson River ferries came long before that. Mr. Smith was off the mark by 64 years.

On October 25, 1931, the George Washington Bridge opened, and the Lincoln Tunnel followed six years later, on December 22, 1937. Both crossings immediately cut deeply into all the ferries' vehicular traffic up and down the river. Trucks, especially, made for the tunnels and bridges. Some commuters changed to buses while others abandoned public transportation altogether and began driving to work.

As early as January 3, 1928, less than two months after the Holland Tunnel opened, the Christopher Street Ferry ceased running after 9 pm and eliminated all Sunday sailings. Saturday schedules were later abandoned too.

World War II intervened and the war effort provided both extra business for the ferries and the death knell for

Traffic waits for the photographer in the westbound tube of the Holland Tunnel shortly after the first vehicular crossing under the Hudson opened in 1927. (Museum of the City of New York)

Hoboken's Upper Ferry at 14th Street. The United States Navy Department wanted to expand the adjacent drydocking facilities and attained a court order to force the closure of the ferry on April 27, 1942, ending 56 years of continual service.

At 23rd Street, the City of New York wanted the Lackawanna to move into the abandoned Erie Slips so the D.L.&W. and Central of New Jersey portions could be torn down to make way for expansion of the Chelsea docks. The railroad balked at the cost needed to upgrade the former Erie facilities, cited their own losses ($150,577 in 1944) and filed for abandonment.

The battle went on for two years, mainly between the local merchants along 23rd Street and the railroad. At midnight on December 31, 1946, what once had been the second busiest transportation terminal in Manhattan closed down forever.

The Christopher Street Ferry, down by 1954 to only 2000 riders a day nearly all of whom worked within walking distance of the ferry, was losing $1000 per day or 50 cents a rider.

A Lackawanna Ferry time-table from the year of the 1939 New York World's Fair showing the front panel, a map of the New Jersey approaches to the three ferries to Manhattan and the normal weekday schedules. Because of passenger complaints about having to come up with four pennies, the foot passenger fare rose to 5 cents in 1935. Coffee and donuts on the upper deck became a regular feature of the ferries' morning runs at this time. (Howard & Suzanne Samelson Collection)

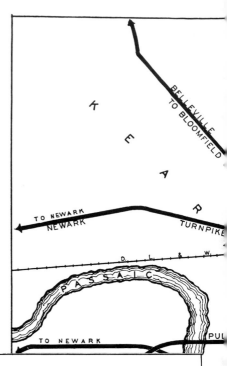

WEEK-DAY SCHEDULES

(See outside page for Sunday and Holiday Schedules)

STANDARD TIME		14th St. Hoboken to 23rd St. N. Y.	23rd St. New York to Lackawanna Terminal Hoboken	Christ. (W. 10th) St., N. Y. to Lackawanna Terminal Hoboken	Barclay St. N. Y. to Lackawanna Terminal Hoboken
Note: From last Sunday in April to last Sunday in September time shown is Daylight Saving Time.		Service Starts	Every	Service Starts	Every
From		5:00a A.M.	30 e	5:15a A.M.	30 e
12:30 to 5:00 A.M.		5:00a A.M.	30 e	5:15a A.M.	30 e
5:00 to 5:30 "		20 a	30 e	30 e	30 e
5:30 to 6:00 "		20 a	30 e	30 e	15 f
6:00 to 6:30 "		12 c	30 e	30 e	15 f
6:30 to 7:00 "		12 c	15 f	15 f	15 f
7:00 to 7:30 "		12 c	15 f	15 f	10 g
7:30 to 7:45 "		7½d	10 g	15 f	10 g
7:45 to 10:00 "		7½d	10 g	10 g	7½d
10:00 to 11:30 "		12 c	10 g	10 g	10 g
11:30 to Noon		12 c	10 g	10 g	15 f
Noon to 1:00 P.M.		12 c	10 g	12 c	15 f
1:00 to 1:30 "		12 c	15 f	12 c	15 f
1:30 to 2:15 "		7½d	15 f	12 c	15 f
2:15 to 3:00 "		7½d	10 g	10 g	15 f
3:00 to 4:00 "		7½d	10 g	10 g	10 g
4:00 to 6:00 "		7½d	10 g	10 g	7½d
6:00 to 6:15 "		7½d	10 g	15 f	10 g
6:15 to 8:30 "		7½d	15 f	15 f	15 f
8:30 to 9:00 "		12 c	15 f	15 f	15 f
9:00 to 10:00 "		20 b	15 f	No Service after 9 P.M. or Sundays	15 f
10:00 to 12:40 A.M.		20 b	30 e		30 e
		No Service after 12:40 A.M. From N. Y.			

a Leave New York: 10, 30, 50 after Hour.
  "   Hoboken: Hour, 20, 40 after.
b   "   Hoboken: 10, 30, 50 after Hour.
  "   New York: Hour, 20, 40 after Hour.
c   "   New York or Hoboken: Hour, 12, 24, 36, 48 after.
d   "   New York or Hoboken: Hour, 7½, 15, 22½, 30, 37½, 45, 52½, after.
e   "   New York: Hour and half Hour.
  "   Hoboken: 15 and 45 after Hour.
f   "   New York or Hoboken: Hour, 15, 30 and 45 after.
g   "   New York: Hour, 10, 20, 30, 40, 50 after.
  "   Hoboken: 5, 15, 25, 35, 45, 55 after Hour.

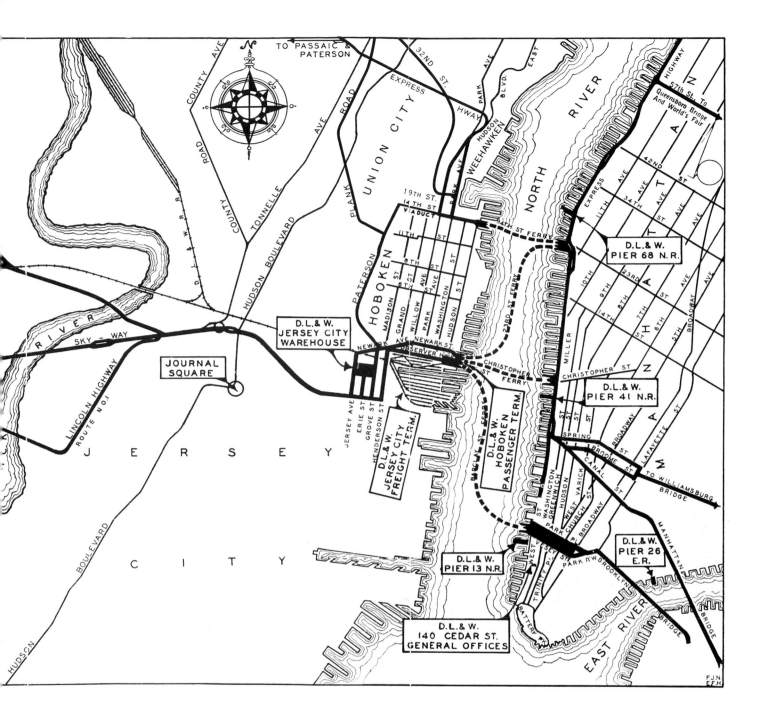

TO PASSAIC & PATERSON

UNION CITY

NORTH RIVER

JOURNAL SQUARE

D.L.& W. JERSEY CITY WAREHOUSE

D.L.& W. PIER 68 N.R.

D.L.& W. PIER 41 N.R.

D.L.& W. JERSEY CITY FREIGHT TERM.

D.L.& W. HOBOKEN PASSENGER TERM.

D.L.& W. PIER 26 E.R.

D.L.& W. PIER 13 N.R.

D.L.& W. 140 CEDAR ST. GENERAL OFFICES

J E R S E Y   C I T Y

HOBOKEN

EAST RIVER

Queensboro Bridge And World's Fair

LINCOLN HIGHWAY

SKY-WAY

HUDSON BOULEVARD

TONNELLE AVE

COUNTY ROAD

PLANK ROAD

Enroute to the 1940 season of the New York World's Fair, Lackawanna 4-6-4 type 1151, renumbered 1940, is shown at Mt. Vernon, N.Y.
(Frank W. Schlegel Collection)

During the abandonment proceedings in July 1954, Paul C. Albus of the Interstate Commerce Commission made this summation: "Diversion of traffic to private automobiles and bus transportation, super highways, decentralization of industry, suburban shopping facilities and a decline in the number of persons attending Manhattan entertainment events because of the popularity of television broadcasts were cited by the examiner as contributing to the decrease in the use of the ferry service."

The meager little group of riders who had offered to pay 50 percent more to keep the ferry, an increase of five cents to 15 cents, must have felt overwhelmed by this evidence, all part of a much larger trend that did not seem at all connected with their own lives.

Christopher Street ferry service ended March 30, 1955, with the ferryboat "Buffalo" making the final run; and the 1876 New Jersey Pavilion brought over from the Centennial Celebration in Philadelphia was taken apart for the last time.

When the Erie merged its ferry service with the Lackawanna in January 1957, and the West Shore Line closed its Weehawken ferry in 1959, that left only the Central of New Jersey ferry from Jersey City to Liberty Street and the Erie-Lackawanna Barclay Street Ferry. And the end was drawing near for the two remaining routes.

By 1962 the ferries carried only 5 percent of the cross-Hudson passenger traffic, down from 10 percent in 1953 and 45 percent in 1930. With both ferry destinations being Lower Manhattan, the ridership had all the characteristics of a pure commuter operation carried to the greatest extreme. Owl service ended on the Barclay Street Ferry on July 22, 1958, and Saturday and Sunday service were eliminated on February 1, 1964.

On the Barclay Street Ferry, a study done by the New York Port Authority in 1963 showed 10,300 persons crossing to Manhattan on a typical weekday, with 9,600

West 23rd Street had six ferry slips for three railroad operations. In this photograph, taken with a box camera from a Lackawanna ferry in the early 1930's, a double-deck Erie ferry occupies one slip and a single-deck Lackawanna ferry signals its departure the right. The three towers in the background from left to right are the Empire State Building, the 23rd Street Ferry clock tower and the spire of the Metropolitan Life Insurance Company at Madison Square. (Homer R. Hill)

The 23rd Street Ferry was about to shut down when this picture was taken in September 1946. Note that the clock face is covered over. Inside a month later, the paint is peeling from the ceiling. Behind the turnstiles to the right is the baggage room. (Both photos - Bill Rau)

In another photograph from the river, the Lackawanna ferry Pocono approaches 23rd Street. To the left is the Marine and Aviation ferry President Roosevelt, used for trooping runs in the harbor during the Second World War, and to the right is the United States Line's Manhattan or Washington. Note the gun mounts on the stern. (Steamship Historical Society, Bill Rau Collection)

The Lackawanna ferry Oswego, formerly the Netherlands (1893), heads into the Christopher Street landing between the old Grace Line Pier 45 and the new Norwegian America liner Oslofjord in the early 1950's. (Steamship Historical Society, Bill Rau Collection)

When the Erie merged with the Lackawanna, the Erie ferry Youngstown (1922) became the Chatham with its bow extended to fit the Hoboken Ferry slips. The Erie ferry Meadville (1936), the last railroad ferry built for North River service shows its distinctive thirties' interior. The Meadville was renamed the Maplewood and had its bow extended too. (Chatham - William H. Ewen, Jr.; Meadville, its interior and Maplewood - Conrad Milster)

A Barclay Street-bound ferry meets one bound for Hoboken just off Lower Manhattan during the afternoon rush hour. (Fielding L. Bowman) **The lucky woman aboard the ferryboat Scranton gets a close look at the liners Santa Paula and France during a crossing from Barclay Street to Hoboken in 1967.** (Fielding L. Bowman) **Not all landings are straight as shown here in the crazy angle the ferry Pocono is taking to enter Slip 3 at Hoboken. To the left is the Binghamton and to the right the Lackawanna and an American Export Line's freighter docked at the Port Authority Piers.** (John S. Dawber, Jr., William H. Ewen, Jr. Collection)

In the final years of the Barclay Street Ferry, the graceful boats shuttled back and forth with fewer and fewer passengers, and were virtually empty during the non-rush hours. The Maplewood, docked in Hoboken, is about to make a morning run while the Scranton slips by in the afternoon headed for Hoboken. (Both photos - Conrad Milster)

One lone passenger walks under the graceful arches along the main deck cabin on the Binghamton. Fortunately, visitors to the ferryboat restaurant Binghamton, moored permanently at Edgewater, New Jersey can still enjoy the simple interiors so popular at the turn of the century. (Jacobsen Collection, Steamship Historical Society)

Three tall stacks and three finely proportioned pilot houses form an elegant line up of the ferryboats Binghamton, Pocono and Maplewood at Hoboken. (William H. Ewen, Jr.)

traveling between 6 am and 10 am, and 7,200 during the one-hour period from 8 am to 9 am. In the reverse direction, a mere 260 ferry riders crossed to New Jersey between 6 and 10 am and only 60 between 8 and 9 am. 95 percent were bound for Manhattan south of Worth Street, mostly walking to their destinations from the Barclay Street Terminal.

The study further reported that passengers chose the ferries over PATH trains if the Barclay Street Terminal was closer to their destination. The difference in transit time between the two modes was minimal, with the ferry crossing taking ten minutes and the PATH nine. The ferries had departures every 7½ to 10 minutes at the height of the rush hour, while PATH dispatched its trains every three to six minutes.

For an equal number of Central of New Jersey commuters crossing the Hudson on their Liberty Street Ferry, there was no alternative PATH service. Instead, the Aldene Plan switched the CNJ trains from the Jersey City waterfront terminal to Newark or ran them directly into Penn Station where most riders, destined for downtown, changed to the subway. The last ferries to Liberty Street stopped on April 25, 1967, just seven months before the Barclay Street Ferry would close.

By the mid-1960's the Erie-Lackawanna was ready to shut down its last ferry. Annual losses, in the days before federal and local subsidies, were running at $500,000, and the fleet of five boats was more than sixty years old, with one, the "Lackawanna," dating from 1891.

The North River is looking particularly gloomy from the top deck and so is the ferry's future. Note the running lights above the pilot house. (William H. Ewen, Jr.)

The Lackawanna, dating from 1891, slides past the Incres Line's cruise ship Nassau, originally built for P & O as the Mongolia in 1923. The ferry Lackawanna will make the last scheduled crossing from Barclay Street to Hoboken at 5:30 pm on November 22, 1967. The Elmira (1905) made the last actual trip 15 minutes later closing out all North River ferry service. Except for the Lackawanna, dieselized in 1949, all the Lackawanna ferries were coal-burning steamers. A stoker fires the boilers on the Elmira in 1961. (All photos - Conrad Milster)

Expensive to operate, too costly to replace and with hulls worn so thin that some captains were afraid a sharp floating object might pierce the shell, they had to go. There was no way to raise the 25-cent fare without sending all but the most loyal ferry riders to the PATH trains.

In the week before the final runs, only 3000 daily passengers remained faithful, not even enough to fill two ferryboats. Only the "Lackawanna" and "Elmira" remained in service. The "Pocono," "Scranton" and "Binghamton" were already withdrawn.

On November 22, 1967, the "Lackawanna" departed Barclay Street at 5:30 pm and fifteen minutes later the "Elmira" followed; and by 6 pm, with the hooks in, over 300 years of cross-Hudson ferry service came to an end, including 156 years of Hoboken Ferry steam operations.

The next morning being Thanksgiving Day, the few travelers off the Erie-Lackawanna trains were directed to a new entrance at the end of shortened Track 1 leading down the stairs to PATH, now their only choice of crossing apart from a local bus to the Port Authority Terminal.

On the newsstands, the *Hudson Dispatch* carried a story quoting the "Elmira's" Chief Engineer, Paul Randall, who had no regrets when he said, "The boat's old. It's old-fashioned. It's obsolete."

Stop engines.

Shortly before the ferryboat Binghamton was sold as a restaurant, she sits in the D.L.&W.'s Brighton Marine Repair Yard on Staten Island. The ferry, damaged by fire as early as 1905 when brand-new, has outlived them all. (Conrad Milster)

CHAPTER V
HUDSON AND MANHATTAN RAILROAD
THE PATH SYSTEM

In the years following the Civil War, railroads became the largest construction projects, and there was almost no place in the country where someone was not planning a rail extension or an entirely new line.

With Manhattan an island, railroad builders focused their attention on spanning the surrounding waters with steel rails to eliminate what were considered cumbersome transfers to ferryboats. Following the first lines that crossed the narrow Harlem River at the northern tip of Manhattan, some thoughts turned to the important Hudson crossing.

In 1874, the first attempts at digging a Trans-Hudson rail tunnel began, only to end in disaster and bankruptcy because the needed technology was not yet there. With the successful completion of the first London tubes under the Thames in 1897, William G. McAdoo, a Georgia-born lawyer with some railroad experience in Tennessee, received enough financing to take over the unfinished tunnels and to begin work again. Using an incline ram pushed by hydraulic jacks called a shield, he made considerable progress in a relatively short period of time.

His venture, by 1905 called the Hudson and Manhattan Railroad, was designed to link three of the New Jersey railroad terminals — the Pennsylvania, the Erie and the Lackawanna— to two direct rail lines under the Hudson into Manhattan. In addition, the H & M would draw passengers from Newark and the Pennsy's new Manhattan Transfer station at Harrison in the meadowlands.

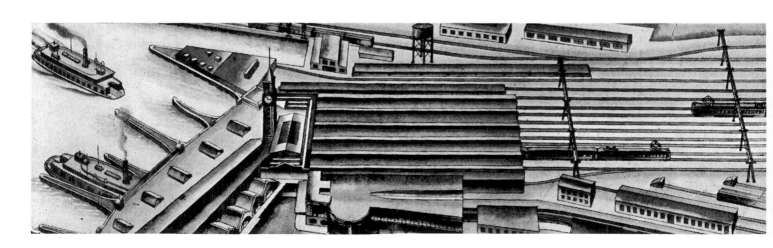

HUDSON & MANHATTAN RAILROAD COMPANY

INCORPORATED UNDER THE LAWS   OF NEW YORK AND NEW JERSEY.

The underwater railroad tunnel opened to the public on February 25, 1908, upon receiving a signal from President Theodore Roosevelt in Washington, D.C. The new subway line ran from New Jersey to 19th Street and 6th Avenue in Manhattan, and by 1910 it reached its present terminus at 33rd Street.

To let its patrons know about the new link to and from Manhattan, the Lackawanna created a new jingle using Phoebe Snow:

Now Phoebe Snow direct can go
From 33rd to Buffalo.
From Broadway bright the "Tubes" run right
Into the Road of Anthracite.

The tunnel to the brand-new Hudson Terminal Building at Church Street in Lower Manhattan opened in 1909, and two years later the system was extended to Manhattan Transfer and Park Place in Newark.

In 1910 the Pennsylvania Railroad opened its own Hudson River tunnels to a monumental new Pennsylvania Station located between 31st and 33rd Streets and 7th and 8th Avenues. A tunnel under the East River for the Long Island Railroad and the Hell Gate line to New England was completed a few years later.

In its first year, 59 million passengers used the Hudson and Manhattan, siphoning off ferry passengers from all the competing lines. The Lackawanna's ferry business remained strong because of increasing commuter business and because some riders found the Manhattan ferry terminals more conveniently located to their place of work. Also, if a Lackawanna Railroad ticket read "New York," the ferry fare was included. In the 1960's turnstiles appeared in the terminal to collect the fare for the ferry separately, and then the railroad tickets read "Hoboken" only.

The H & M carried its highest volume of passengers in 1927 when 113,141,729 used the subway-style trains. The completion of the Holland and Lincoln Tunnels took away some of the traffic and the Great Depression even more. By 1954, only 37 million passengers used the H & M, and it declared bankruptcy.

A common stock certificate for 50 shares features a North River scene under which is running, free of the heavy water traffic, a Hudson & Manhattan tube train bound from New Jersey to the Hudson Terminal Building on the right. The Pennsylvania Railroad's Exchange Place Terminal is prominently displayed because the PRR was part owner of the H & M. (Joel Lipman Collection)

This ornate capital with the letter "H" for Hoboken has been painted over many times since the H & M station opened in 1908. (The author)

A 1908 post card showing the entrance to the brand-new Hudson & Manhattan Railroad tunnels at Hoboken Terminal. (Howard Samelson Collection).

A second post card shows passengers using the mezzanine level. (Howard Samelson Collection).

The train platforms at the Hoboken Terminal in 1908. Travelers today will note the letter "H" embossed on the capitals atop the supporting columns. (Howard Samelson Collection).

At Manhattan Transfer in the New Jersey Meadowlands near Harrison, the first Hudson & Manhattan tube train has arrived from Church Street, Hudson Terminal on September 27, 1911. Passengers changed to and from Pennsylvania Railroad trains on the new line to and from new Penn Station in Manhattan. (Port Authority of New York & New Jersey)

The 19th Street and 6th Avenue Station was the original terminus of the uptown H & M line until the completion of the station at 33rd Street. 19th Street closed when the platforms at 14th and 23rd Streets were extended to handle longer trains, but the curious can still see the now darkened station when traveling the line. This photograph as taken just a week after the H & M opened for business. Note the smartly dressed young men besides the fare boxes and the spitoon on he floor. (Port Authority of New York & New Jersey)

In a deal that allowed the New York Port Authority to construct the World Trade Center, that agency, on September 1, 1962, assumed complete control of the Hudson and Manhattan Railroad, reorganizing it as the Port Authority Trans-Hudson Corporation — PATH as it is generally known today.

Considerable capital investment, including a new fleet of cars, and a relatively low fare brought the annual ridership up to 54.6 million (1984), with the PATH trains handling 70 percent of the cross-Hudson rail traffic.

The H & M/PATH caused the gradual decline of ferry ridership over a 59-year period, until boat service ended entirely when the Erie-Lackawanna closed down Barclay Street on November 22, 1967.

The recent fare increases on PATH are designed to inject some much-needed money into a system that needs a complete overhaul and more rush-hour capacity. Weekday ridership averages 200,000 and is rising.

The Holland and Lincoln Tunnels and the George Washington Bridge crossings are oversaturated with traffic, with peak-hour delays averaging 30 minutes. It is highly likely that history will come full circle to make use of Trans-Hudson ferries again. The questions are when and where.

The open door of a modern PATH train operating between "HOB" for Hoboken and "WTC" for the World Trade Center. (The author)

CHAPTER VI
THE TERMINAL IN DECLINE
PARTIAL RESTORATION

Age, changing tastes, urban decline and a marked shift in transportation use contributed to the Lackawanna Terminal's long slide into shabbiness and decay.

Arriving immigrants began bypassing Ellis Island and the barge transfer to the terminal for more direct clearance at the Hudson River piers and at the airports. Some new arrivals would still trickle across to the regular trains for a while, however.

The famous harbor beacon, the Lackawanna Terminal clock tower, had its copper sheathing torn off in high winds and soon was declared structurally unsafe and dismantled. Today a nondescript communications tower rises from the roof.

World War II blackout regulations required that the skylights in the upper ferry concourse and the Tiffany glass ceiling in the main waiting room be tarred over. The famous restaurant, beset with declining patronage, especially New Yorkers coming across the river, closed about the same time.

The New York Society of Model Engineers established a popular model train layout in the unused portions of the upper ferry concourse. However, they were forced to vacate when the post office shifted the mail-handling facilities from the cramped quarters on the south side of the terminal to the team concourse and upper ferry concourse opposite slips 1 through 4. The post office then gradually cancelled the mail contracts all over the country, especially in the late 1950's and

In this aerial view of the Hudson River, a small New York Central ferry looks to be escorting the giant Cunarder R.M.S. Queen Mary to her West Side berth in 1956. Note the active car float operations between the finger piers on the Manhattan side. The Lackawanna Terminal is in the lower right-hand corner and the new Port Authority piers, the reason for the photo being taken, are dead center. (Port Authority of New York and New Jersey)

early 1960's. As the Lackawanna train consists lost their mail and express cars, the railroad was allowed to drop its money-losing long-distance fleet from the timetables. The empty mail-handling space is of cavernous proportions.

With the passing of the long-haul trains, the baggage room closed. All the conductors, trainmen and engineers working the remaining commuter trains could go home at night, and the Railroad Y.M.C.A. shut its doors.

When the Barclay Street Ferry stopped, the pedestrian traffic through the main waiting room dropped off, and the lunchroom became the operating crews' lounge to rest in between trains. Other railroad employees had offices in the immigrant building and in a portion of the upper ferry concourse and the old restaurant. A small area behind the former doors leading from the waiting room to the team concourse became a ''Lost and Found'' and ''Parcel Check.''

Buses replaced trolleys; and they no longer needed to make a loop in front of the ferry bays, releasing that space for employee parking. The Public Service trolley trestle came down in 1949, and the trolley terminal that abutted the Y.M.C.A. was replaced by a simple shed for buses.

In 1978 computer-operated Solari indicator boards showing train times, track numbers and destinations superseded the old departure signs and the colored light system at the track gates. At a glance, a commuter on the run had been able to find his Pascack Valley Line train by looking for two yellow lights, a Main Line or Bergen Country Line train indicated by two white lights or a Boonton Line train with one white and two red lights. Vertical lights indicated Lackawanna trains and two rows of horizontal lights, Erie trains.

One light system that still functions shows a green light when a World Trade Center train is arriving at the

lower level and a yellow light if the train is coming from 33rd Street. The stationmaster can hold a departure a couple of extra minutes to allow connecting passengers to make their trains.

The passage of time and lack of maintenance allowed the copper facade to deteriorate and the ferry bridges to drop into the river. The terminal's roof began leaking, and the broken pipes running within the iron columns holding up the Bush Train Shed corroded the capitals and flooded the platforms.

The situation was grim enough for transportation officials to call for the terminal's demolition by the end of the 1960's, and it nearly happened. Hoboken's entire waterfront had fallen into disuse with the arrival of container shipping technology that sent the oceangoing freight traffic to other sections of the port and made the car float facilities redundant. Manhattan's situation was not much different, except for small pockets of activity associated with passenger shipping, excursion traffic and the banana import trade.

Also taken in 1956, this aerial view is generally south with no less than six North Street ferries on the move. The one in the center would be an Erie Railroad boat turning toward the Pavonia station. With the heavy river traffic, the ferries had quite a lot of maneuvering to do to make it across and maintain the tight schedules. In the foreground are the extensive freight and passenger yards belongng to the D.L.&W. (Museum of the City of New York)

A couple of U.S. mail trailers are backed up to the post handling facility in front of the ferry house. When this photo was taken in the late 1950's, only the Barclay Street Ferry still operated. The sign "Erie (out of sight) - Lackawanna Hoboken Terminal" now reads "NJ Transit Hoboken Terminal." (Conrad Milster)

Passenger shipping moved from Hoboken back to Manhattan, if it survived at all. Here the elderly Greek liner Neptunia, built way back in 1920 as the Dutch Johan de Witt, rests after a transatlantic voyage at Pier 1, Hoboken in April 1953. This pier would soon be demolished to make way for more modern cargo handling facilities. In the accompanying picture, passengers of all ages are guided by posted taxi rates. Most of the destinations listed here are railroad stations along the New Jersey waterfront and in Manhattan. (Both photos - Port Authority of New York and New Jersey)

A "Western Electric" car rests during the weekend at the upper level trolley terminal in Hoboken on January 7, 1943. The shed had one inbound and three outbound tracks. (Arthur C. Ward)

A Public Service car climbing the trestle from Hoboken to Jersey City on August 6, 1949. (Collection of Railroad Avenue Enterprises).

A line-side view of the Union City car with Hoboken and the Manhattan skyline in the background on the next to the last day of operation. The line would permanently close on August 7, 1949. (Collection of Railroad Avenue Enterprises).

The ferry slips are sadly neglected with the facade and transfer bridges literally dropping into the river. The letters "Erie" were added at the time of the merger in 1960. (The author)

The Jersey Central Terminal is undergoing an impressive restoration to restore it to its 1889 look. One of the major changes saw the ferry house torn down in 1983 exposing the original terminal building the way that no one alive today would have remembered. The terminal sits amidst Liberty State Park, accessible by local bus from Journal Square and by car, but sadly no longer by train or ferry. The "aerial" view is from the World Trade Center. (Both photos - the author)

Edward Thoden, Engineer Structures, seen here atop the Lackawanna Terminal, has worked with the railroad since 1951. His generous help allowed the author to inspect virtually the entire building, from a terrifying walk on narrow boards across the waiting room skylight to the underside of the terminal at water level. (The author)

When developers began to eye Manhattan's underutilized property, such controversial ideas as building an interstate highway down the West Side came into favor. In return, developers promised riverside parks, although it is questionable how well-maintained they would be, given the state of some of the city's other major open spaces.

In Hoboken, planners and builders wanted to demolish what was considered to be an outdated transportation terminal and replace it with a smaller railroad station connected to a high-rise office building.

Preservationists considered the historic structure to be far too valuable to lose, and they mounted a campaign to designate the Lackawanna Terminal as an official landmark. The Hoboken Environment Committee, a local citizens' group and one of the prime movers in saving the terminal from the wreckers' ball, was successful in having it placed on the National Register of Historic Places in July 1973.

Developers still eyed the terminal's unused space, but most of their attention turned to the former Port Authority piers just north of the terminal.

Plans were drawn to make improvements to the busy railroad station and to repair and restore some of the terminal's fine architectural features. With a $4.8 million grant from the Federal Economic Development Administration, the restoration began in earnest in 1978. An additional sum of $160,000 for ornamental work came from the State Office of Historic Preservation.

Outside, repairs to the copper facade were made to the front of the main waiting room, to the former Y.M.C.A. building and to the ferry house canopy. In areas not visible, other materials were used, and most of the abandoned ferry house was left entirely alone.

Major work on the waiting room roof allowed for the complete restoration of the Tiffany glass ceiling. Tarred

Three miscellaneous pictures show one of the heavy iron lamps outside the terminal's waiting room, two doorknobs with the letters "LR" in Edward Thoden's office and a restored capital in the train shed. (All photos - the author)

The waiting room today is the most interesting and well preserved section of the terminal's interior spaces. The cream cover chosen for the iron work on the staircases and the false balconies contrasts with the dark paint scheme used in the original design. The letters for "Lunch Room" and "Restaurant" are in blue glass. A modern electric water cooler (since removed) has taken the place of the lion's head and his basin. The Tiffany Glass ceiling fifty feet up is the jewel that gives the waiting room its special feeling. (All photos - the author)

85

over during the Second World War, each pane of colored glass was carefully removed, cleaned and put back. Only four small pieces needed replacing.

Inside the waiting room, the walls, floors, windows and benches were given a thorough cleaning and all ornamental plaster and iron work was painted.

Unfortunately, the additional illumination makes some of the tacky concession stands and modern additions even more evident. Telephone booths line a portion of one wall and a water cooler blocks the original fountain showing the face of a lion. The clock on the west wall was not replaced, nor were the four huge chandeliers or the small lights buried in the plaster ceiling. However, the overall effect is spacious and pleasing, and only those who are aware of the original plan will know that certain pieces are missing.

The waiting room's somewhat faded beauty and grandeur can best be appreciated by standing on the landing at the top of the stairs. The people seated on the high-back wooden benches and others standing on line to buy train tickets look small indeed. To the left, at the same level as the landing, was a pedestal holding a model of one of the original D.L.&W. locomotives from the middle of the 19th century.

The roof above the long train concourse, once covered by wire mesh glass, is now punctuated by clear bubble-style skylights providing more natural light than ever. Beyond the train gates, the Bush Train Shed, tracks and platforms have received most of the restoration money, because of their serious state of deterioration and vital transportation function.

The canopy roofs were rebuilt without the old wire mesh skylights. A new drainage system has the pipes running down the back side of the iron columns, rather than through the hollow shaft, to avoid the repetition of rusting. Most but not all the ionic capitals were re-

A workman replaces the copper facade on the terminal's south side. The other photos show the rich ornamental design no longer visible, outside the former restaurant and on the terminal's roof. (All photos - the author)

placed, not by iron but by a cheaper fiberglass material. Only with close scrutiny can one tell the difference. Lack of funds prevented restoration of the capitals at the far end of the long platforms.

The train platforms were reconstructed and the track beds renewed to allow proper drainage during periods of rain.

At a ceremony on October 3, 1981, New Jersey Governor Brendan T. Byrne and state transportation officials rededicated the Lackawanna Terminal, the significant event forming part of the first annual Hoboken Renaissance Festival.

Railroad memorabilia dealers, food vendors and transportation displays draw tens of thousands of people every year, filling the place with more humanity than even Kenneth Murchison would have ever thought possible.

While the Lackawanna Terminal will never return to its pristine 1907 condition, there is much to admire in the fine detail work that remains and in its function as an efficient passage through which 70,000 people pass every day to and from Manhattan.

In early 1984 restoration began on two of the ferry slips, for show and maybe one day to reopen a passenger ferry service to Manhattan. Additional work has recaptured the public plaza that surrounds the altered position of the statue of Sam Sloan. In the long-vacant section of the upper ferry concourse, NJ Transit has built new offices.

The Lackawanna Terminal should have a long and successful run.

The East River ferry Welfare (1930) that once ran from East 78th Street to Welfare, now Roosevelt Island, has had a new lease on life as the restaurant Drifters I, first in Providence as the Victoria, and since late 1983 next to the Hoboken Terminal (since foundered). The plaza here filled with railroad employee cars was reconstructed into a park. In the background is Stevens Institute of Technology, started by the Stevens family who got Hoboken going in the first place. (The author)

CHAPTER VII
NJ TRANSIT AND HOBOKEN TERMINAL

On July 16, 1979, NJ Transit became the sole owner of the Hoboken Terminal; and on January 1, 1983, at 12:30 a.m., NJT took over complete control of the terminal's commuter operations and several bus routes. NJ Transit inherited a railroad with a remarkably good reputation under Erie-Lackawanna ownership, but one that had slipped somewhat with Conrail, the federal government corporation that reluctantly took over the commuter operations through default.

NJ Transit's aggressive leadership is demonstrating a sincere desire to improve service on all its bus and train routes throughout the state with capital improvements to the infrastructure, new equipment, heavy promotion of its services and good public relations.

The result had been increased ridership on all rail lines except for the Morristown Line, where re-electrification construction temporarily disrupted service. In the Hoboken District the diesel-operated Pascack Valley Line, the Bergen County and the Main Line have more train service, with additional schedules within New York State on the line to Port Jervis.

There are plans for the Boonton Line, also diesel-operated, to be connected to the end of the Montclair Branch. If that occurs, ridership should increase substantially.

On the Morristown Line and Gladstone Branch, the electrified full-service portion of the Hoboken operations, the long delay in changing from 3000 volts DC to

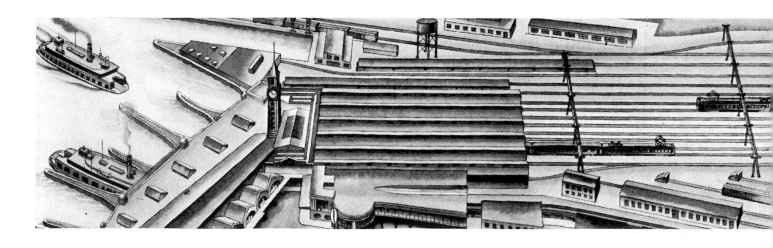

On May 24, 1983 a pair of Gladstone Branch trains line up at Bernardsville, with the left one bound for Gladstone and the right set originating here for Hoboken. This line featured a private club car service, one of the last of its kind in commuter service in the country and even receiving a mention in the Preppy Handbook. **During re-** electrification work, diesel-hauled trains often ran under the wires as seen here at Gladstone in June 1983. A U-34-CH is about to depart for Hoboken with a pair of Comet I cars over a route that passes through some of the most scenic country in the metropolitan area. (Both photos - Homer R. Hill)

Kevin Kearns, trainmaster, led a tour of the old terminal tower where 155 levers control the switching operations in the Hoboken train yards. During the rush hour, a director barks orders to three lever men who adjust the positions and repeat the orders at the same time.
(All photos — the author)

25,000 volts AC caused a marked drop in the passenger figures. The ancient electric fleet's declining reliability, poor timekeeping and longer schedules sent many commuters to their cars or onto buses.

However, the long-awaited 1984 completion of the re-electrification scheme has reversed the decline, with faster and more frequent schedules using relatively new Arrow III electric cars serving freshly spruced-up stations.

During the weekdays most of the Morris and Essex Line traffic is headed to Lower Manhattan, though significant numbers take the PATH to 33rd Street for midtown destinations. On weekends, nearly all trips are made to midtown for shopping and recreation, and Hoboken is less well sited than the Port Authority Bus Terminal. Consequently, while the Morristown Line and Gladstone Branch maintain weekend services, the Suffern Line has only Saturday service and there are no weekend trains at all on the Boonton and Pascack Valley Lines.

Future plans call for some trains to run into Penn Station via a track connection at Kearny where the M & E parallels Amtrak's Northeast Corridor. Diesel line service would have to continue to operate into Hoboken, though perhaps an electric shuttle train could make a connection into New York.

The new terminal tower's commanding presence overpowers the MU storage yard, and to the right, the cripple track, in this view taken from the old D.L. & W. travelling carne. (Howard Pincus) **The tower, a tall brick structure, replaces the old tower seen in the distance.** (The author) **A Morristown electric stands next to a soon-to-be-unveiled signal, controlled by the new tower in August 1984.** (Howard Pincus)

The Hoboken Terminal is served by Route 63 NJ Transit buses to the Port Authority Bus Terminal and Route 21 to Fort Lee as well as by local service on Washington Street. Maria Transportation operates one of the oldest units, 30X, dating from the late 1950's. (Both photos - the author)

With the river right under foot and the winds blowing off the Hudson, Ellen Greening, stationmaster, displays her winter uniform, helps out a passenger, checks her watch to make sure the gate gets closed on time and poses with trainman Bill Campbell during the height of the rush hour on January 14, 1981. (All photos - the author)

Two moody scenes reflect the end of an era. In September 1980, the bright sun reflects off a string of Morristown electrics as another train arrives to board passengers at the beginning of the rush hour. A year later on a wet July afternoon, a set of electrics awaits an assignment for later in the day. (Both photos - the author)

A young man is deep into his reading just prior to departure from Hoboken while homebound commuters are beginning to fill the seats of another MU still marked "Erie Lackawanna" in the summer of 1984. (Both photos - Howard Pincus)

A diesel-hauled train of Pullman Standard coaches dating from 1971 - 1973 is about to start its push-pull run on one of the former Erie Lines on October 3, 1981. (The author).

Rush-hour trains are just minutes apart in this listing on the computer-operated Solari Board in the train concourse. While the new year was already 14 days old when this picture was taken in 1981, "Seasons Greetings" still dominates the 'remarks' column. (The author)

Towards the end of the rush hour in June 1977, a Gladstone bound train leaves Hoboken Terminal. (Fielding L. Bowman)

A new Arrow III and older Morristown Line electrics are being worked on in the MU shed in Hoboken on August 17, 1984. (Howard Pincus) This Gladstone branch train of Arrow III's heralds the beginning of the long-awaited new era for Morris and Essex Line commuters. (NJ Transit)

On an average weekday in early 1984, the Hoboken District handled 249 trains, dropping to 77 on Saturdays and 43 on Sundays. The monthly total comes to about 5750 trains. More weekday and weekend trains were added to the Morris and Essex Line in September 1984, following re-electrification.

The seven-year NJ Transit projections show a 25 percent increase in rush-hour ridership, with the largest gains on the Morristown Line and Gladstone Branch, the result of re-electrification and greatly improved service.

With the vehicular tunnels and the bridges at the point of strangulation during the peak periods of the day, more commuters need to be encouraged to use mass transit into the city, and New Jersey Transit's rail operations appear to be eager and ready to handle the business in a most energy-efficient way.

BIBLIOGRAPHY

BOOKS, GUIDES & STUDIES

Appleton's Dictionary of New York, D. Appleton and Company New York, 1902.

Bonsor, N.P.R., **North Atlantic Seaway,** Volume 1, David & Charles, Newton Abbot, 1975; Volumes 2-5, Brookside Publications, Jersey, Channel Islands, 1978-1980.

Hardy, A.C., **American Ship Types,** D. Van Nostrand Company, Inc., New York, 1927.

Historical Transactions 1893-1943, The Society of Naval Architects and Marine Engineers, New York, 1945.

King's Handbook of New York City, Moses King, Boston, 1893.

McAdoo, William G., **Crowded Years,** Kennikat Press, Port Washington, NY, 1931.

Origin and Destination Study, PATH and Trans-Hudson Ferry Passengers, The Port of New York Authority, December 1963.

Perry, John, **American Ferryboats,** Wilfred Funk, 1957.

Roberts, Franklin B. and Gillespie, John, **The Boats We Rode,** Quadrant Press, New York, 1974.

Smith, Harry J. Jr., **Romance of the Hoboken Ferry,** Prentice-Hall, Inc., New York, 1931.

Taintor's Route and City Guide, City of New York, Taintor Brothers, New York, 1867.

Transit and Transportation, Regional Plan of New York and Its Environs, New York, 1928.

NEWSPAPERS

Frank Leslie's Illustrated Newspaper, Hudson Dispatch, Hudson Observer, Jersey Journal, Jersey Observer, Newark Star-Ledger, New York Herald, New York Herald-Tribune, The New York Times.

PERIODICALS & SMALL PUBLICATIONS

American History Illustrated, "Eight Minutes to New York," August 1974.

The Bicentennial Comes to Hoboken, John J. Heaney, 1976.

Block Line, October 1981, A Comprehensive History of Hoboken Terminal, Frank Reilly, Tri-State Chapter of the National Railway Historical Society.

Bush Train Shed, Lackawanna Railroad Terminal, William B. Barry, Jr., New York, 1909.

Engineering News, The New Terminal Station and Ferryhouse of the Delaware, Lackawanna and Western Railroad, Hoboken, N.J., Sept. 20, 1906.

Erie-Lackawanna — Historic Structures Report, Patricia Florio, Hoboken, New Jersey, May 1982.

50th Anniversary 1931-1981, Suburban Electrification, Delaware, Lackawanna & Western R.R., Wes Coates, Electric Railway Publications, October 1981.

Jersey Central Lines, Hoboken Terminal Renaissance, Wes Coates, Jersey Central Railway Historical Society, Inc., October 1981, Clark, N.J.

New Jersey Business, "On the Waterfront," September 1983.

New York, New Jersey, Port and Harbor Development Commission, Chapter 19, Ferries and Vehicular Tunnels, 1920.

The Official Guide of the Railways, etc., National Railway Publication Co., New York, various dates.

The PATH Gazette, February 25, 1983, Port Authority of New York and New Jersey, Harold M. Lewis et al.

Steamboat Bill, "The Hoboken Ferries," Graham T. Wilson, Spring and Summer 1979, Steamship Historical Society of America.

Tidewater Terminals of the Erie Lackawanna Railway, William Sheppard, 1976.

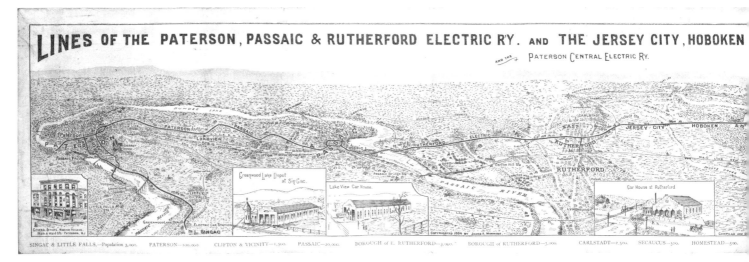